HANGING *the* MIRROR

The DISCIPLINE of REFLECTIVE LEADERSHIP

Alan Scheffer • Nancy Braun • Mark Scheffer

Wasteland Press

www.wastelandpress.net
Shelbyville, KY USA

Hanging the Mirror:
The Discipline of Reflective Leadership
by Alan Scheffer, Nancy Braun, and Mark Scheffer

First Printing – September 2012
ISBN: 978-1-60047-758-4

Printed in the U.S.A.

0   1   2   3   4   5   6   7   8   9   10   11

This book is dedicated to the many sincere leaders with whom we have worked and grown.

Table of Contents

INTRODUCTION

It is our conviction that business leaders today, seeking both personal development and organizational improvement, need to be challenged far more than they need to be trained or taught.

In our 25 years of consulting work numerous leaders have told us that they have been trained to death over the course of their careers. They say that they have learned various management systems, adopted diverse approaches, and yet seen little change in the fundamental dynamics of their organizations. They tell us, often with more than a hint of cynicism, that they have lost faith in such programs.

The reason this scenario plays out again and again is, we believe, quite simple. Most leadership development focuses almost exclusively on surface-level behaviors, giving tools, tips, and strategies designed to improve leaders' performance. What such approaches fail to take into account is the fact that action is invariably shaped by deeper paradigms, mental models, and value systems. Trying to change daily actions without addressing these underlying factors – as so many training programs seek to do – becomes an exercise in futility. Some level of short-term change can be achieved, but as enthusiasm inevitably wanes, ingrained habits and patterns of thought begin to reassert themselves. It becomes clear that the linchpin of sustainable leadership development – and therefore productive organizational change – is transforming not what leaders do, say, and decide, but what they believe, feel, and assume. The key, in short, is not what leaders do, but who leaders are.

The term "reflection" as we will use it in this book refers to the process by which all of us can become increasingly aware of the contours of our own thinking and reasoning. Learning to better identify and assess the beliefs, attitudes, and assumptions that give rise to our daily patterns of behavior is crucial to any process of ongoing transformation. It is also the central aim of this book.

Reflective leadership, then, can be thought of as the related processes of gaining both self-knowledge and self-mastery, with the goal of becoming an ever more effective leader of people. This discipline, which we call "hanging the mirror," involves:

1. Candidly identifying the values and beliefs that shape our behavior

2. Objectively comparing those values to what is known through research about the practice of leading people effectively

3. Assessing our moment-by-moment leadership choices to determine what kind of assumptions and beliefs those choices reveal

4. Rethinking beliefs that run counter to tested knowledge, and replacing them with different and more knowledge-based choices

Hanging the Mirror is divided into several main sections. Chapters one through nine concentrate on individual leaders and the elements of a personal process of reflection. Chapters ten and eleven widen the scope of focus, addressing the challenge of making an entire system more reflective. And the final chapter explores in greater depth the nature of reflection as a "discipline" – an ongoing and long-term practice to which one commits him- or herself.

Our intention is for this book to be a practical tool that leaders can return to again and again in their efforts toward ongoing development. To that end, we have included questions to guide reflection at the end of every chapter. These provide a starting point for exploring both the principles presented and one's own beliefs and values related to those principles. Some of the questions can be answered on the spot. Others might become clear after a few days' thought. But most will require sustained attention and honest self-assessment over a period of months or even years. This is the nature of true reflection.

As we mentioned before, our consulting work has focused not on training or coaching leaders, but on challenging them. We have tried to retain that sense of challenge in this book. But hard as we may sometimes push, it is important to acknowledge that we do so not as experts holding the "answers" but simply as fellow travelers walking a common path of development. In the end, we, like you, are simply human beings trying to come to a better understanding of what it means to work in collaboration with other human beings.

Please join us in taking this journey.

Hanging the Mirror: It's All About You

1

In the early years of our consulting work, a CEO asked why he should fly us to San Diego instead of hiring a local consultant. Why, indeed, we thought, and began putting the question to long-time clients. Their responses provided ample food for thought, but one stood above all the rest. "You got us to stop looking at each other and start looking at ourselves," said the president of one organization. "You pushed each of us to hang a mirror and really take a look at what we saw."

As human beings, we all have our own mirror, our own capacity for mindfulness and reflection. This is a universal birthright, a defining feature of the humanity we share. But how many of us use this mirror to consciously and conscientiously assess our attitudes and behavior, and refine their impact on those with whom we come into contact on a regular basis?

Reflection is key to success, regardless of aim or activity. The athlete who fails to analyze his jump or throw will be hard pressed to improve his game, just as the teacher who neglects to ponder why students invariably struggle with a certain unit has little hope of seeing improved comprehension in the future. The process of dispassionately observing ourselves, analyzing the habits and behaviors we see, and revising those actions is critical to achieving sustainable improvement. Only if we know what we are doing – and avoid becoming enmeshed in the mirage of what we think we are doing or wish we were doing – can we hope to better our performance.

All of us engage in reflection. We do it every time we formulate a plan and later look back to consider how well it served us. The question is how often we dig into more personal and interpersonal areas of reflection. How might our behavior be straining relationships with our children? How are our daily actions impacting interactions with our employees and coworkers? How faithfully are we living up to the ideals we champion with our words?

Reflection on personal conduct is needed in many aspects of life, but perhaps in none so much as leadership. Leaders, by definition, exercise authority over other people. That power invests their behavior with added weight and gives their reflection (or lack thereof) particular importance. Authority is what makes individuals leaders, but reflection – on-going, honest, and objective reflection – is what makes them effective leaders. It is the features of this ongoing reflection, the dynamics and challenges you will face in your efforts to walk a path of reflective leadership, that this book will address.

> *Reflection on personal conduct is needed in many aspects of life, but perhaps in none so much as leadership.*

Why Leadership Matters

Years ago a group of Harvard Business School faculty considered a deceptively unassuming question: What leads to a prospering service organization? What elements are essential to building an outstanding enterprise and how do those elements relate to one another? Turning to best-practice strategies gleaned from industry-leading businesses, they set out to discover and document a "new economics of service." But in the process, they ended up encountering a new and striking vision of leadership, a vision expressed "in terms rarely heard in corporate America."

Their analysis, published in *Harvard Business Review* under the title "Putting the Service-Profit Chain to Work," was no ode to touchy-feely management. Directed at practical-minded leaders, it sought to put "hard values on soft measures" so managers could target investments for maximum competitive impact. Nevertheless, their work revealed a thoroughly organic system steeped, at every level, in the humanity of its participants. "Anyone who looks at things solely in terms of factors that can easily be quantified is missing the heart of business, which is people," remarked one CEO quoted in the research. It is people who design products, people who produce them, people who sell them, and people who purchase them. Business, it becomes clear, does not merely involve humanity, it *is* humanity. And the more clearly leaders can understand how feelings, perceptions, attitudes, and beliefs (their own included) impact organizational performance, the more effectively they can build cultures of excellence.

Given the rigor and insight of this research, it is worth reviewing its key points and implications for a reflective leader.

The Impact of Loyal Customers

The Harvard group began by designating revenue as the bedrock of a healthy, thriving organization. A prospering business, they said, must generate enough income to support expansion, development, and continued growth. Even nonprofits and committedly mission-oriented organizations must secure revenue – whether from profits, donations, user fees, grants, or endowments – if they are to retain talent and achieve real-world results.

With that foundation in place, the first question became: what aspects of organizational functioning lead to the healthiest possible revenue stream? In answer, the group suggested that the *quality* of market share, measured in terms of customer loyalty, can influence profitability just as much as the *quantity* of share. Citing statistics estimating that a 5% increase in loyalty can increase revenue 25 to 85%, they demonstrated that the repeated patronage of loyal customers was a powerful source of lifetime revenue.

The loyalty they described was no small thing. Far outstripping common conceptions of preference or brand loyalty, it implied a depth of relationship in which "customers [are] so satisfied that they convert the uninitiated to a product or service." So fervent was this devotion that the study referred to customers who displayed it as 'apostles' of a given organization.

Organizations that seek loyal customers, however, must first create consistently satisfied customers, the research found. Customer satisfaction emerged as the next link in the chain, but years of records tracking it on a five-point scale revealed a surprising twist. While 'satisfied' (level four) and 'very satisfied' (level five) customers might seem similar, the data showed a great, almost exponential, difference in loyalty. Such was the disparity that in one case, level-five customers were found to be six times more likely to repurchase equipment than level-four customers. These 'very satisfied' customers were those hard-won apostles whose loyalty often meant a lifetime of business.

Quality Isn't Enough

If satisfied customers lead to loyal customers and loyal customers lead to increased revenue, what leads to customer satisfaction? The answer, the study found, lay in creating value for customers, the value that comes from providing a consistently high quality of product and/or service.

All of us form impressions of value by comparing the costs we pay, both monetary and otherwise, with the results we receive. Price is critical to these comparisons, but so are perceptions of quality. A higher-priced mechanic might strike us as a better value than a comparably-skilled competitor simply because he is unfailingly friendly and willing to answer questions. A certain computer might seem to offer more value than a lower-priced equivalent because of its reputation for durability and reliability.

Quality is therefore central to perceptions of value, but to influence consumer behavior that quality must be uniform and dependable. It cannot be left to chance. If some experiences with a company are excellent, but others are mediocre or downright unpleasant, customers will rightly feel their satisfaction is not a priority. From the customer's point of view, quality and service are either consistent or they are nonexistent. A car that runs without problems nine days out of ten is not 90% acceptable, it is 100% unreliable. Similarly, an organization that leaves your experience as a customer up to chance deserves little acclaim. You might not object to the fact that your experience depends on the store location you visit or the employee who answers your call. You might even declare yourself satisfied with the organization. But you would not feel any particular affinity for it, nor would you go out of your way to recommend it to others. For organizations to distinguish themselves and create true customer loyalty, value must, in the eyes of customers, be delivered first time, every time.

The Role of Employees

Such standards of quality and value point squarely to employees as the next link in the chain. Employees – typically those at the very lowest levels of the organizational hierarchy – are the means by which services are delivered and products produced. They are the point where an organization's many policies, plans, and procedures culminate in a customer experience that is good, bad, or simply unmemorable. It is little surprise, then, that the Harvard group found that quality and value depended most directly on employees' productivity, loyalty, and ownership of their work.

Each of these closely interrelated factors is important in its own right. Productivity enables more work to be done in less time with less waste. Loyalty ensures that hard-won skills and relationships are not lost to turnover. But employee ownership – the feeling of doing one's own work as opposed to handling tasks assigned by the boss – is perhaps the most fundamental of the three. Ownership is the difference between investment and indifference, between working to accomplish something meaningful and working simply to receive a paycheck. It is the feeling of having a personal stake in something, and years of research have linked it to a range of salutary effects such as enthusiasm, productivity, loyalty, morale, and commitment.

All of us want to have responsibility over the work we do. We want to be able to *achieve* something, rather than just follow other people's directions. This is a truth, backed by the Harvard research, that suggests that the workplace condition employees value above all else is "the ability and authority . . . to achieve results for customers." But this truth can also be easily validated through our own work experience. We all want ownership of the tasks that fill our days. When our organization allows such ownership, we work productively and strive to give our best because the work we do is ours, and not someone else's. And when it does not allow such ownership – and many do not – we throw up our hands and do only what is required to stay out of trouble.

Just as loyal customers must first be satisfied customers, the service-profit chain shows that employees with ownership over their work must first be satisfied with their job and position. Job satisfaction has long been an aim of many managers, but satisfaction, important as it is, is far from an end itself. Satisfied employees are, of course, preferable to dissatisfied ones. But just as satisfied customers were only a shadow of those "very satisfied" customers six times more likely to repurchase equipment, merely satisfied employees will never rival those who take active ownership of their work. To deliver consistent, exceptional quality and service, satisfaction is important, but ownership is imperative.

Culture: The Invisible Impact

Leaders long to see ownership, loyalty, and productivity in the systems they lead. They value it in workers and seek it in applicants. But while these qualities find expression in the conduct of individual employees, the most effective leaders know they are too important to be left to individual disposition. Ownership and investment must be woven into the fabric of an organization. They must be made a part of organizational culture.

Take a moment to think about the notion of culture. Derived from the Latin *colere*, "to cultivate," it is a concept steeped in overtones of development and growth. In microbiology a culture is the medium in which a tissue grows and reproduces, the means by which development becomes possible. In food production a culture is that essential element that transforms milk into yogurt and juice into wine. Culture in this sense is vital, dynamic, and unfailingly alive.

Taken in the social sense, culture is just as vital. How projects are viewed, how information is shared, how departments interact with one another, how mistakes are handled, how questions are received – all these are expressions of organizational culture. Defining everything from how crises are handled to how coffee breaks are taken, culture makes organizations what they are. So pervasive is its influence that virtually no facet of organizational performance remains untouched by it.

Perhaps nowhere is this more apparent than in the attitudes of employees. In the service-profit chain, the Harvard group pegged the health of an organization's culture to the views and perceptions of its employees, writing that the quality of a work environment is "measured by the feelings that employees have toward their jobs, colleagues, and companies." They further noted that this environment is "characterized by the attitudes that people have toward one another and the way people serve each other inside the organization."

Leaders tend to attribute behavior and attitude to individual employees, but culture plays a powerful role in shaping workplace dynamics. A social service agency we once worked with, for example, had absorbed a small provider of similar services. Because the organization being acquired was free from many of the problems – criticism, negativity, backbiting – that plagued the parent organization, the partnership created considerable excitement. But all too soon the fresh attitudes and excitement began to disappear as the new staff came into contact with the old. "In the beginning they were so positive and constructive," one executive said with a weary sigh, not six month after the start of the partnership. "Now they're just like us."

Culture can bring out the best in workers, but it can also destroy model employees. The difference between average organizations and outstanding ones, then, is not one of personnel but of culture.

Culture – those shared norms, values, expectations, and ways of getting things done that characterize an organization or workplace – changes people. It can bring out the best in workers, but it can also destroy model employees. Culture is what determines the human resources a leader has to work with as well as the organizational performance he or she will be able to achieve. The difference between average organizations and outstanding ones, then, is not one of personnel but of culture.

The Wake of Leadership

We once ate in a restaurant with exceedingly good service. When we told our waitress how impressed we were, she replied without hesitation, "Oh, that's the manager. He's always talking about customer service, having meetings about it, encouraging us. It's really important to him."

Though only a few years into the workforce, this young waitress already knew what the authors of the service-profit chain found in their research: that workplace culture can always be traced back to the decisions of leaders. Far from a phenomenon arising of its own accord, culture is the inescapable product of leadership behavior and choices. It is established by leaders' every question and remark, shaped by their every decision and offhand comment. It is the byproduct of their organizational authority, the wake of their leadership.

Whether they realize it or not, leaders are creating culture at every moment of every workday. They could not stop if they tried. The challenge, then, is not how to build workplace culture, but how to guide what is already being built, how to shape it into something beneficial and vigorous. We sometimes tell our clients that culture can be likened to a leader's back yard. With attention and effort, the potential of the land can be harnessed to produce beautiful flowers and delicious fruits. But if the plot is ignored or neglected, the problem is not that nothing will grow there. The problem is that anything and everything will grow there. Without care and attention, the yard will become choked with the vegetation of seeds blown in from the outside world, bits of garbage tossed in by passers-by, and undergrowth planted years ago which has spread unchecked ever since. It will become a hodgepodge of the counterproductive, the inconsequential, and the fortuitously beneficial.

> *Whether they realize it or not, leaders are creating culture at every moment of every workday. The challenge is how to shape it into something beneficial and vigorous.*

The issue then becomes how leaders can best build productive cultures, how they can ensure their yard is helping them instead of hindering them. Things like organizational structure and design, internal systems and policies, and formal statements of philosophy, mission, and values have their place, says Edgar Schein, one of the foremost authorities on workplace culture. But he and others suggest that the day-to-day behaviors employees see exhibited by their leaders are far more influential determinants of culture. What leaders pay attention to and measure, how they respond to organizational crises, the things they coach and model are what truly determine the contours of a working environment, they say. A vision statement describes what leadership wishes a culture to be; their daily behavior determines what it actually is.

Workplace culture is a force leaders cannot afford to underestimate. Approached with determination and intentionality, it can instill in employees ownership, satisfaction, and attention to quality. But if culture is haphazard and personality-driven (as in many organizations), its effects can range from apathy and underachievement to dysfunction and calamity. So potent are its effects that Schein went so far as to suggest the possibility that "the only thing of real importance that leaders do is to create and manage culture."

This is a dramatic, almost revolutionary reframing of the role of leadership. Leaders know they are responsible for bottom line tangibles like patrons served, beds filled, units sold, and dollars earned. Many know that these factors depend on issues of quality and value. But because many are unaware of the power of organizational culture to create the employee ownership and investment that lead to consistent quality and value, they resort to strict oversight or elaborate systems of quality control. They end up relying on micromanagement, which is as inefficient as it is ultimately self-defeating.

Leaders are indeed responsible for results, but they best achieve these results not by the eagle eye of managerial oversight, but by creating a culture in which employees are enthused about the outcomes they are pursuing. In short, excellence of product, service, and human performance depend first, foremost, and beyond all else on excellence of culture.

A Responsibility of Every Leader

Leaders are constantly creating organizational culture, continuously shaping a working environment that does or does not lead to employee ownership and enthusiasm, that does or does not conduce to quality service and superior products, that does or does not ensure an outstanding customer experience. Culture building is therefore a prime target for leadership reflection and analysis. "Most people take culture as a given," remarked one CEO in the service-profit chain article. "It is around you, the thinking goes, and you can't do anything about it. However, when you run a company, you have the opportunity to determine the culture. I find that when you champion the noblest values . . . employees rise to the challenge, and you forever change their lives."

But true as these words are, culture is not just the responsibility of senior leadership. Every person with supervisory oversight determines culture for the people he or she oversees. Every shop foreman and care manager, every crew leader, site supervisor and front-line manager shapes the organizational environment of his or her direct reports. To achieve organizational excellence, then, every leader – and not just the person in the corner office – is obliged to reflect on the culture he or she is building day in and day out. Are you, as a leader, consciously directing your efforts toward a culture of service or innovation or compassion? Are you intentionally making decisions that reinforce a productive working environment? Or are you simply accepting whatever culture happens to evolve in the workplace? Your organization may survive the latter. It may carry on, and few may complain. But far, far more is within reach.

Reflection in Practice – One Simple Question

That leaders determine culture and that culture determines performance is clear. Leaders create the conditions that influence whether risk is embraced or avoided, whether questions are valued or discouraged, whether information is shared or hoarded. They do this not through any inherent superiority, but simply because of the organizational authority they hold. Authority is the primary distinction between bosses and employees – it is arguably the *only* distinction between them – and the way a person exercises that authority determines in large part how effectively he or she will lead.

In our years of consulting we have found that the answer to one question will tell a great deal about the culture that exists in an organization. That question is: To what extent do leaders use their authority *for* employees or *on* them?

Organizations in which employees feel that leaders use their authority for them – protecting them, facilitating their work, supplying them with resources – are usually focused, cohesive, and optimistic about the future. Organizations in which employees feel that leadership uses its authority on them – isolating them, intimidating them, using their work to further personal agendas – are usually characterized by resentment, apathy, and conflict.

Personal and ongoing reflection on this one simple question – how you exercise your authority as a leader and to what ends you turn it – is a cornerstone of the process of hanging the mirror.

Questions to Ponder – Culture

- How would I describe the culture in which my employees work? How would my employees describe it? In what ways do our views differ?

- In what ways am I creating culture every day? What are my primary impacts on my organization's culture? What could I do or stop doing that would improve the culture?

- Is our culture distinguished by its excellence? Does it bring out the best in people? What conditions do I consciously create that cause employees to bring their best to the workplace?

- To what extent do I use my power and authority *for* my employees versus *on* them? How would my employees answer this question?

What You Believe: The Foundation of Behavior

2

Much of what we think of as the business of doing business – striking deals, formulating plans, launching initiatives – takes place in the external world. Tangible activities fill our days and constitute the prism through which we view and understand our life. But while such external engagement consumes our time and attention, business authorities, academics, and thinkers have long suggested that the most fertile field for leadership attention is the inner world of values and understandings. Time and again they have suggested that importance be placed not only on what leaders do, but on how they think and what they believe. Here, they say, are the fundamental criteria by which we act and react. Here is the source of decisions both large and small. Surely it is not insignificant that the first special-issue edition in the 79-year history of *Harvard Business Review* was themed "Break-through Leadership: Why Knowing Yourself is the Best Strategy Now."

Every action you take as a leader is a direct reflection of the values, attitudes, beliefs, and mental models that constitute your personality.

Putting these ideas in slightly different terms, it can be seen that what you do is a reflection of who you are. Every action you take as a leader is a direct reflection of the values, attitudes, beliefs, and mental models that constitute your personality and essence. Every behavior you manifest, every goal you pursue, every choice you make is directly shaped by some element of who you are.

The connection between internal being and external engagement is of extraordinary importance. To understand why, think about the best and worst bosses you ever worked for. Undoubtedly there were differences in what they said and did, but most people, if given a little time for reflection, will say that the real difference lay in their thinking and values. Behaviors, actions, and approach are important, but it is the internal landscape that ultimately informs behavior, molds actions, shapes approaches and determines the effectiveness of leadership.

As true as this is for our supervisors and leaders, it is equally true for us. In whatever leadership capacity we operate, the influence exerted by our internal makeup is enormous. Our conceptions of work, responsibility, loyalty, obedience – the list is endless – shape the minute by minute choices we make in interacting with employees, conceiving policies, and making leadership decisions. Becoming an effective leader, therefore, involves more than strategies and approaches. It requires seeing ourselves for the human beings we truly are. Reflective leadership involves getting to know ourselves at a

> *Becoming an effective leader requires seeing ourselves for the human beings we truly are. It involves willingly and committedly making a practice of doing what we usually do only when demanded by external requirements.*

level most of us do only when forced by difficult circumstances. It involves willingly and committedly making a practice of doing what we usually do only when demanded by external requirements.

Above and Below the Line

For years our seminars included an exercise that explored the basic requirements of exceptional communication. The exercise asked participants to think of the best listener they had ever known and describe what made that person a good listener. Most of the responses it generated centered on active listening techniques like maintaining eye contact, asking clarifying questions, and mirroring body language. But without fail someone would raise a hand and say that the most important feature was that the person "sincerely cared about me."

We gradually realized that this response and others like it were qualitatively different from the rest. Genuinely caring about someone was not a skill to be practiced. Wanting the best for a friend or coworker was not a technique to be employed. Answers of this kind, we grew to understand, were not things that people did but rather things that they *were* – things they stood for and believed in.

As we realized that the exercise was eliciting not one but two sets of responses, we began separating them with a simple horizontal line. Above the line we recorded the surface-level actions, skills, behaviors, policies, techniques, and procedures that came to participants' minds first and fastest. Below the line we noted the attitudes, assumptions, beliefs, paradigms, and values that were not so immediately obvious, but which constitute far more core elements of personal identity. This fundamental delineation evolved, over time, into a model of human nature and behavior that, while simple, has proven invaluable to leaders striving to hang the mirror.

From a functional standpoint, the model's utility comes not so much from separating the external "above-the-line" world from the internal "below-the-line" world, but from clarifying the relationship between the two. Above-the-line is where the rubber meets the road, where action is taken and results begin to show. It is where the world is engaged. Below-the-line is a sphere that is less visible but arguably more important, for it is from below the line that actions and behaviors receive their direction and impetus. Putting this in leadership terms, above-the-line is what you do as a leader, below-the-line is why you do it.

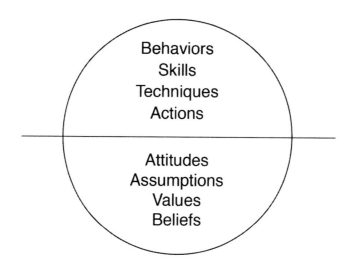

Understanding the relationship between these two gives valuable insight into the dynamics that are daily shaping organizations. The often-seen struggles of leadership training provide an apt example. The reason so many such initiatives fail to achieve significant change is simple: training is frequently approached entirely above-the-line. Aiming to teach new leaderships skills or techniques, it rarely gives attention to surfacing, exploring, and reframing those below-the-line factors upon which current behaviors rest. Unfortunately, such focus all too often results in leaders who, upon completion of training, can pass a test on the subject material, yet fail to operationalize new skills and behaviors in a sustainable way.

The above-and-below-the-line model allows leaders to move from flash-in-the-pan approaches to more lasting change initiatives. It gives leaders insight about why trying to change behaviors without an honest exploration of the below-the-line attitudes and assumptions that support them is a losing proposition. It also empowers them to investigate the drivers of their own behavior, sometimes revisiting life-long attitudes or surprising themselves with unsuspected biases. These insights make leadership development far more sustainable and give leaders a powerful tool for continuous improvement.

Examples of Above and Below the Line

Douglas McGregor, former professor at the MIT Sloan School of Management, was one of the first business authorities to clearly articulate the power of below-the-line mental models and beliefs. His Theory X/Theory Y model provided one of the earliest illustrations of how leadership thinking impacts leadership behavior. Central to this model were a set of propositions which McGregor felt were representative of the attitudes that determine the success of organizational culture and performance. The following statements are derived from those propositions:

1. The average human being can find work a source of satisfaction.

2. Most employees have the capacity to exercise a relatively high degree of imagination, ingenuity, and creativity in the solution of organizational problems.

3. Man does not need external controls or the threat of punishment, but will exercise inner self-direction and self-control to attain organizational objectives to which he is personally committed.

4. The potentialities of the average human being are far above those that are typically recognized in organizations today.

5. Under proper conditions, the average human being in an organization learns not only to accept but to seek responsibility.

6. For many organizational tasks, managers can rely on the individual to exercise self-control.

7. Even the lowliest untalented laborer seeks a sense of meaning and accomplishment in his work.

8. Most employees are capable of exercising a certain amount of autonomy and independence on the job.

9. In most organizations one can generally trust one's subordinates.

10. Giving greater independence to most employees would be good for the organization.

Propositions like these probe fundamental beliefs about human nature, beliefs that define the contours of one's approach to leadership. Participants in our workshops have, without exception, indicated that they would work with excitement, enthusiasm, and commitment for a leader who held these beliefs. In fact, they say that they would be happy to work for such a leader *without knowing anything else about that leader.* Why? Because when push comes to shove, we all know that actions conform to attitudes in the long run. We know that if a leader believes even some of the statements derived from McGregor's propositions, his or her decisions, actions, policies, and interpersonal relationships will invariably be based on trust, mutuality, and the value of the human element in the workplace. Similarly, we know that a leader whose below-the-line beliefs are contrary to those principles will naturally create a work environment that is authoritarian, untrusting, and micromanaged.

Improving your effectiveness as a leader, then, requires you to reflect not only on what you do and accomplish, but on what you believe and value.

Improving your effectiveness as a leader, then, requires you to reflect not only on what you do and accomplish, but on what you believe and value, for your views of employees and their role in the workplace will determine your leadership of them, for better or worse.

What We Believe Versus What We *Think* We Believe

It is easy to wax eloquent about the importance of beliefs and mental models, easy to nod along and think *yes, yes, what could be more obvious.* Actually digging into the specifics behind those generalities, however, is far more challenging. The drivers of our behavior are so integral to our worldview that they are transparent, almost invisible to us. Why do we act the way we do? It turns out to be surprisingly difficult to say.

Part of the difficulty stems from the way we think about our behavior. People act in accordance with "maps" of what they believe to be true about the world, mental maps that allow them to plan, implement, and evaluate actions in a rational manner. These mental models are indispensable to our cognitive functioning, but they have a significant catch: the maps that shape our behavior are often not the ones we *think* shape our behavior. Chris Argyris and Donald Schon, of the Harvard Business School and MIT, wrote extensively on this dichotomy between what they called *espoused theories* and *theories-in-use*. Espoused theories, they said, are those values and beliefs to which we consciously subscribe and that we express to others. Theories-in-use, on the other hand, are the things that actually determine our behavior, the worldview and values that are revealed by our actions.

Espoused theories and theories-in-use can be the same, but often are not. We once heard the manager of a body purification center being interviewed in a bustling morning diner. The woman spoke with eloquence and conviction about the benefits of restoring systemic balance, releasing flows of energy, and ridding the body of destructive toxins. Her interviewer, however, observed that she was smoking a cigarette and eating a plate of greasy sausage. "How does that square with ridding the body of toxins?" he asked. The woman was silent a moment, then laughed and said, "Well, you gotta wake up somehow, right?"

The woman's espoused theories – the beliefs, values, and views she consciously championed – clearly centered on the importance of alternative, holistic health. Her behavior, however, suggested a more complex theory-in-use. Such differences could be mistaken for hypocrisy, but Argyris and Schon were clear that both espoused theories and theories-in-use are sincere expressions of genuine belief. One simply determines behavior and one does not. The classic example is the manager who steadfastly champions the cause of employee empowerment while micro-managing in daily practice. Though some might pay mere lip service to the idea of delegation, most managers honestly support it and think they practice it. It just happens that, in actual fact, they do not. The strength of their espoused theory fools them into thinking that their behavior is something other than what it really is.

We were once presenting these concepts in a seminar when the CEO of a heavy-equipment manufacturing firm started from his chair and hurried out of the room. Returning a few minutes later, he explained that though he profoundly believed that all employees were trustworthy partners in a common enterprise, he had scheduled time clocks to be installed on the floor of his factory that very day. Despite the egalitarian beliefs he espoused, he realized that his actions revealed a theory-in-use that factory workers could not be trusted as fully as office workers. Dismayed and unwilling to accept the double standard implied by his behavior, he had stepped into the hall to cancel the installation.

Because all of us sincerely believe the values we espouse, we rarely spot contradictions within ourselves. Biased toward a logical and consistent view of our actions, we tend to see about what we expect to see in our behavior. But just as we clearly see the disconnects in others – the "open door" supervisor who hates interruptions, the "give me honest feedback" associate who prickles at constructive

> *Because all of us sincerely believe the values we espouse, we rarely spot contradictions within ourselves.*

criticism – they see the discrepancies in us. They spot the contradictions we habitually overlook, but they also know coherence between expressed beliefs and actions when they see it, and they know how rare and valuable it can be.

A Searching Reexamination

The previous chapter demonstrated that workplace culture stems from leadership choices. Given that these choices are shaped and driven by below-the-line realities, the dynamics identified by Argyris and Schon pose at least two challenges to the reflective leader.

The first regards the validity of the espoused theories we hold. We must first determine whether the things we consciously believe lead to the results we think they do. Does competition between employees really increase productivity? Does collaborative leadership really lead to better decisions? Do low level employees really need constant supervision? These are questions to which we must give serious attention, for if the principles we consciously champion are not sound, our leadership will inevitably flounder. These questions will be addressed in more detail later in this book.

The second, subtler issue concerns the degree to which our behaviors match the theories we espouse. We all assume that the theories we espouse are the theories we actually use, that the things we consciously believe are reflected in our actions and choices. The challenge is this: that all of us act in ways we might not realize and conform to standards we might not consciously support. The line between espoused theories and theories-in-use is a slippery and beguiling one, and rarely if ever do we consider, like the woman in the diner, how easily the one can be mistaken for the other.

As leaders, we can address these issues only by taking an honest look at daily behaviors and reflecting on the attitudes and beliefs those behaviors imply. Only by stepping back from ourselves can we note that our tendency to act unilaterally doesn't match our championing of collaboration, that our pattern of pitting supervisors in competition with each other doesn't support our speeches about teamwork, that our level of information sharing contradicts what we think we believe about open communication. Only by a searching reexamination of ongoing patterns of behavior can we begin assembling a picture of the values, paradigms, and assumptions that give impetus to our actions and form to our decisions.

> *Only by a searching reexamination of ongoing patterns of behavior can we begin assembling a picture of the values, paradigms, and assumptions that give impetus to our actions and form to our decisions.*

Maintaining this level of awareness throughout a day – while sitting in meetings, chatting with coworkers, writing reports – takes effort. It is *work* in the truest sense of the word. Moreover, it almost invariably punctures some of the comfortable fictions we build around ourselves. Maybe you realize that instead of never having time to talk with subordinates, you simply do not value their opinions that much. Maybe you find that though you think of yourself as being available to coworkers, you actually wish they would more often resolve problems themselves. Maybe you discover that though you wish others would shoulder more responsibility, you are reluctant to give up the opportunity to be the hero. Such revelations can be hard to face, particularly when they run counter to familiar assumptions and cherished self-conceptions. But simply becoming aware of these disconnects is no small achievement, and beginning to grapple with them is a step of real growth, not only as a leader, but as a human being as well.

Warren Bennis, founding chairman of the Leadership Institute at the University of Southern California, once wrote that learning to be a leader is virtually the same process as becoming an integrated and healthy person. Leadership, he implied, cannot be divorced from an individual's core identity. It cannot be separated from the grit and fiber of who he or she is. Reaching down to our roots, leadership is an expression of our inmost selves, and only by understanding that inner reality can we hope to master the personal decisions that daily define ourselves and our organizations.

Questions to Ponder – Below-the-Line

- What fundamental beliefs, attitudes, and assumptions shape my leadership philosophy and approach? How is my thinking reflected in my leadership actions?

- How open am I to the possibility that my attitudes and beliefs contribute to organizational difficulties?

- Which of my leadership actions and decisions might contradict the values and principles in which I say I believe? In what areas do the people around me, especially my employees, see contradictions between what I say and what I do?

- What could I do or stop doing to bring my actions more into conformity with my stated values? What below-the-line thinking would need to change in order for my actions to be more aligned with my stated values? How willing am I to take on those changes?

Defining the Mirror: A Framework for Reflection

3

Think a moment about mirrors. Mirrors allow us to examine our physical appearance, to check traffic around us, to get a perspective we would not otherwise have. They are the tools we use when we want to ascertain how closely our idea of the world fits with what is really out there.

The mirror we hang in a leadership sense serves much the same purpose. Facilitating observation and contemplation, it enables us to match our suppositions to the world as it is. It provides a means to evaluate our behavior and hold ourselves accountable to standards, both our own and others'. But where physical mirrors are easily understood, the mirror we use to reflect on leadership behaviors and choices is less obvious. Its constituent elements are numerous, but three – knowledge, choice, and perception – are crucial to effective leadership. Leaders must understand that their success rests not on personal preference or style but well-tested principles; they must consistently and mindfully choose those principles; and they must validate those choices through the perceptions of their employees and coworkers.

These themes of knowledge, choice, and perception comprise central elements of the mirror by which we must evaluate our leadership performance. Are we respecting the known principles of

Knowledge, choice, and perception comprise central elements of the mirror by which we must evaluate our leadership performance.

effective interaction? Are we choosing actions that reflect those principles? Do other people perceive us to be choosing those actions? These questions each hold their own challenges, and each deserves sustained consideration and thought.

Knowledge

People are often promoted to leadership through technical knowledge or performance – a talented line cook replaces a retiring sous-chef, a go-to programmer heads a newly created team. Once there, however, these new leaders' duties require human competence as well as technical ability. No longer is someone simply a machinist, she is a machinist supervising other machinists. Where previously she had only to master technical duties like milling, grinding, and lathing, she now must establish effective channels of communication, resolve disputes, build culture, and master a host of other people-related skills. With promotion into leadership, the knowledge base required of her doubles, and a strictly technical base of knowledge is no longer sufficient.

Leadership is every bit as knowledge based as skilled trades and technical professions. It requires an understanding of the management of the systems, structures, and processes of any organization. Yet it also requires competence in the human knowledge base, that fundamental body of knowledge about how human beings act, react, and interact. If leaders' actions reflect this human knowledge base, the systems they lead will prosper. If their actions violate its principles, they will face chronic difficulties.

Respecting the Human Knowledge Base

We all understand the role of knowledge in daily life. We know that if the recipe calls for four hours at 250 degrees, we can't cook the roast at 500 degrees for two hours and expect tender meat. We know that we cannot leave houseplants outside over the winter in a cold climate and expect them to live. We understand that we cannot violate the principles of a knowledge base without consequences, and we choose our actions accordingly.

Unfortunately, our expectations are very different when it comes to the human knowledge base. Though it makes no more sense than putting a cake in the freezer and expecting it to come out piping hot, almost all of us violate the human knowledge base day after day and still expect our systems to function productively. Illogical as it is, this mindset can come

If leaders' actions reflect the human knowledge base, the systems they lead will prosper. If their actions violate its principles, they will face chronic difficulties.

to characterize not only individual leaders, but entire organizations. We undermine others but expect their support. We criticize subordinates but expect them to offer ideas and input. We stick to ourselves but expect others to communicate information to us. In other words, we treat others any way we see fit, and wonder why our systems are plagued with dysfunction.

In one of our seminars, a supervising nurse once said that she always followed a knowledge base in her medical duties because it was the only way to effectively treat and care for patients. But while she consciously applied a knowledge base to dispensing medicine and cleaning wounds, she said she now realized that when she acted as a supervisor of other nurses, she didn't base her behavior on knowledge at all. Instead, she based it on her mood, how much time she had, what kind of pressure she was under, or whether or not she liked the person with whom she was dealing. This insight, she said, was a wakeup call and gave her an idea of the importance of the discipline of reflective leadership.

Leadership and Personality

In presenting the features of the human knowledge base, the question of leadership style often arises. How does a firm reliance on the human knowledge base take into account variations in manner and approach? How are basic human differences accounted for?

Because leadership is a personal undertaking, leaders will always reflect, to some degree, a vast range of personality. This is natural. But what leaders must understand, what they cannot afford to misconstrue, is that style never justifies violating the principles of the human knowledge base. Professional chefs employ a vast range of culinary styles, but they must all cook meat to the same temperature to kill harmful bacteria. They must all heat milk gradually to keep it from scorching. They must all conform to a common knowledge base, regardless of personal style or approach.

Leadership, like cooking, can accommodate a range of styles, but like cooking its fundamental principles supersede philosophy or preference.

Leadership, like cooking, can accommodate a range of styles, but like cooking its fundamental principles supersede philosophy or preference. A leader might be naturally introverted, but the performance of his staff will suffer if he does not give sufficient feedback. A leader might be naturally exacting, but employee morale will plummet if she indulges in unconstructive criticism.

Regard for the human knowledge base, then, is crucial to reflective leadership. As leaders work to identify and ponder their below-the-line attitudes, assumptions, and beliefs, research-based knowledge provides a trusted standard by which to evaluate, question, and potentially reframe leadership thinking. It provides objective research in light of which leadership behaviors and habits can be appraised.

Choice

As critical as regard for the human knowledge base is in building effective human systems, knowing something doesn't guarantee that we will act on that knowledge. All too often we leaders can articulate principles that define outstanding organizations, but the systems we lead do not manifest those very principles. We know most of what we need to be doing, but often we are not choosing – day by day, moment by moment – to act on that knowledge.

As critical as regard for the human knowledge base is in building effective human systems, knowing something doesn't guarantee that we will act on that knowledge.

This is perhaps the central challenge facing leadership at all levels: the practices we know to be constructive are not consistently applied, while the habits we know to be detrimental continue unabated. Do any of us really believe that sarcasm is conducive to productive meetings? That interdepartmental turf battles contribute to an efficiently functioning organization? That withholding information from perceived rivals leads to the best possible solutions? Yet these dynamics are rife in the workplace, from the largest multinationals to the smallest family businesses, and without leadership reflection they proliferate unchecked, sapping the strength from our organizations every day.

A World of Choice

Leaders often feel handcuffed by circumstances beyond their control. Stifling policies, dwindling resources, and countless organizational challenges leave leaders feeling they are at the mercy of forces greater than themselves. No one likes the feeling of constraint or impotence, but the truth is that as leaders we *are* powerless in many ways. There is much that lies beyond our sphere of influence. But while we have little choice over what happens to us, we have almost unlimited control over how we respond. We live in a world of choice.

The capacity for choice was a central theme of Viktor Frankl's seminal work, *Man's Search for Meaning*. Frankl, an Austrian neurologist, psychiatrist, and Jew, spent three years in the Theresienstadt concentration camp in almost unimaginable conditions. But as awful as the experiences he faced were, they taught him that no amount of hardship could take away a person's freedom of choice. The Jews imprisoned with Frankl all shared the same circumstances, but they chose very different responses, he said. Some gave up hope; some resigned themselves to death but worked to alleviate the suffering of their neighbors; some did whatever it took to survive. Regardless of their decisions, they all retained the power of choice, Frankl said.

This concept is quite straightforward intellectually. Unfortunately, it turns out to be devilishly difficult to put into practice. In large part this is because reactions can become so deeply engrained in our emotional circuitry that they seem automatic. *That guy just rubs me the wrong way*, we say, or, *Those meetings always make me feel stupid.* Talking about how we lost our temper like a set of keys or blew our top like the gasket of a faulty engine, we externalize the source of our reactions and in doing so give others the power to "make" us angry or discouraged. We relinquish control over our frame of mind and rarely give thought to the disadvantage we then face – putting us, in a very real way, at the mercy of others.

This is a personal problem, but it can be an organizational one as well. Leaders strive to build optimum workplace culture, but behavior born in the heat of the moment rarely exemplifies the best practices of the human knowledge base. Because organizations are shaped by leadership choices, the less control leaders have over their own reactions, the less able they are to build effective workplaces.

An Act of Mindfulness, an Act of Will

Picture a sumptuous buffet filled with dishes and platters of every size and description. Visualize the tables and sideboards, the pitchers and bowls. Now imagine that instead of being covered with food, this buffet is overflowing with choices, with every possible response to any imaginable situation, be it verbal, emotional, or physical.

This is the buffet of choice, a metaphor that illustrates the vast array of reactions from which we choose at every moment of every day. The buffet is our constant companion, and every time we receive any external stimulus we pick *something* from the table. Maybe we grab a handful of "smile politely and tune out." Maybe we pour a glassful of "lend a hand where I can." Maybe we take a bite of "ignore it and hope it goes away." Maybe, as one of our associates said she did during a strained exchange, we reach out and, from every possible reaction, choose "get really pissed off." We are free to take what we like, but we never leave the buffet empty-handed. We always choose our reactions, whether we realize it or not.

The metaphor is a simple one, but it highlights two elements that are central to productive and knowledge-based choices. The first is mindfulness. Leaders must first become mindful of the innumerable occasions for choice presented by their daily interactions. They must remain aware of their options, the vast spread waiting on the buffet, and they must reflect on their power to choose from among them. But they must also exercise the volition to actually *make* the productive choices available to them. They must act on what they know. They must exercise will.

Making consistently productive choices is a deceptively challenging form of self-mastery. Choosing to advance the greater good even when one is upset, distracted, frustrated, tired, or indignant takes attention and commitment. It is *work* in the truest sense of the word. But organizations are only as good as the choices of their leaders, and the thousands of routine choices we make throughout a day have large,

> *Making consistently productive choices is a deceptively challenging form of self-mastery.*

even transformational consequences. Just as mountains are ground down by the steady trickle of unassuming streams, the many small choices leaders make day in and day out are what ultimately define an organization and its culture.

The theme of personal choice is a powerful one, both within and outside the workplace. We once worked with an association of newspaper publishers. One publisher spent his lunch break pacing an empty hallway. After more than an hour, he finally approached us. "This theme of choice is shocking," he said. "I've always known I had choice – choice over who to hire and fire, over what to publish or reject. But I'm beginning to understand that every day I am surrounded by choices I don't even see. Every time I pass an employee in the hallway, I have choice. I can smile, nod, frown, look away, pull out my phone, stop to chat, or anything in between. That's amazing." He pondered a moment, then added, "And you know what? The same thing is true when I'm with my eight-year old son."

> *Organizations are only as good as the choices of their leaders. The thousands of routine choices we make throughout a day have large, even transformational consequences.*

Perception

Say a leader does everything so far considered in this chapter. Say she owns responsibility for her role in shaping workplace culture. Say she delves into the human knowledge base and works to internalize the components key to building a superior functioning organization. Say she diligently works to align her choices with the principles and guidelines of the human knowledge base. This leader is making all the right moves, but her work is still not done. Why? Because solitary contemplation will never transcend personal biases and yield a true reflection of the world. Only when self-reflection incorporates the views and perceptions of others, only when we reach beyond our own beliefs and expectations, can it be said that we have truly hung the mirror.

The issue of perception is tricky because while we human beings can assess our impact on others to a degree, our perceptions will be necessarily one-sided, no matter how sincere. We can strive for impartiality, can do our best to put ourselves in other's shoes, but we will get only so far. Think about your boss and his relationship to you. Though he might honestly

> *Only when self-reflection incorporates the views and perceptions of others can it be said that we have truly hung the mirror.*

put thought into how his decisions affect you and your work, he will never understand the consequences of his actions as fully as you do. His assessment will always be, at best, limited. Any leader's would be.

To illustrate this point, let us share an example often used by one of our associates. Imagine that you wanted to know what kind of husband this man is. How might you find out? You could ask him directly, but that would only reveal the kind of husband he thinks he is, or tries to be, or hopes to be. If you wanted to know what kind of husband he actually is, he says, you would do far better to ask his wife. She is the one who interacts with him as a husband on a regular basis, and her perspective is uniquely positioned to assess his efforts. Her perceptions are the true test of whether he is being as effective a husband as he thinks he is. In the workplace self-reflection must take into account the views of employees. Just as comedians know that audience reaction is what determines the quality of a joke, leaders must learn that the views of employees – and not their own perceptions – are what determine the quality of workplace dynamics. You may think you are an approachable supervisor, but if your employees think otherwise, communication will be poor. You may think you treat subordinates equally, but if they perceive favoritism, cohesiveness and teamwork will suffer. You can describe the kind of leader you think you are or are trying to be, but only your employees can say what kind of a leader you actually are. If you want to be effective with them, then, it is their view that must concern you.

Because employees behave and produce according to their own perceptions of the world – and not those of their employers – their perceptual framework must be taken seriously indeed. This does not mean that leaders are obliged to accept everything employees think, nor does it mean that leaders must agree with all employees' views. What it does mean is that leaders are obliged to invest employees' views with as much legitimacy as their own and refuse to dismiss perceptions contrary to their own as "just what they think."

> *You can describe the kind of leader you think you are or are trying to be, but only your employees can say what kind of a leader you actually are.*

Reflective leaders must also account for the effect of organizational authority on perceptions. Though the difference between you and your subordinates might seem relatively insignificant to you, that difference of authority matters a great deal to them and underlies your every interaction together. No matter how close you feel to them, your authority ensures that they steer clear of your hot buttons, walk carefully when you are having a bad day, and tell you things in ways you will find most palatable. And because they do this without telling you, only if you look carefully will you spot the shadow your authority casts. To benefit from their honestly-held perceptions, then, you must manage the effects of your own authority by actively working to drive fear out of the workplace, not by dismissing the caution employees feel as a natural byproduct of your organizational authority, but by taking these feelings into account as you ask for people's openness.

Taking Stock of Yourself

Reflective leadership is a process of taking stock of ourselves, of objectively looking at our actions, our beliefs, and our espoused theories and theories-in-use. Knowledge, choice, and perception, taken collectively, constitute the mirror by which this takes place.

As an example, if we take the question of whether we use our authority for people or on people, we must first ask ourselves how our below-the-line beliefs stand up against knowledge. If we believe, at least in part, that authority can rightly be used on people, the knowledge base will challenge the legitimacy of that view and hopefully begin a process of reevaluation and reframing.

If our belief matches the knowledge base, that authority should be used for and not on people, the issue becomes one of choice. Is our belief a theory-in-use that is reflected in our day-to-day choices? Or is it merely an espoused theory that begins and ends in words alone? Only to the extent that our beliefs are realized through conscious choices do our organizations benefit from them.

Perceptions are the last element of the mirror, the culmination of the knowledge we consult and the choices we make. All of us mistake espoused theories for theories-in-use on occasion, but the people around us see only the behavior being shaped by our theories-in-use.

Reflective leaders make a point of seeking out the perceptions of others. In this regard it is important for leaders to create an environment that employees perceive as safe and welcoming of feedback.

All of this requires discipline. Practicing on-going reflection takes effort – not in bursts of enthusiasm or short-lived good intentions, but over the long haul. Exploring, reexamining, and sometimes changing long-standing below-the-line attitudes and beliefs

> *Practicing on-going reflective leadership takes effort – not in bursts of enthusiasm or short-lived good intentions, but over the long haul.*

demands exertion. But mindfully reflecting on one's choices and behavior is a habit of central importance. Few of us would consider driving an eighteen-wheeler on a busy interstate without side view mirrors. Yet leaders routinely head complex organizations with no conscious mechanism of reflection. Moreover, many never even consider the possibility they might need it. This is a reality that should give every leader pause for thought.

Questions to Ponder – Knowledge, Choice, Perceptions

- How much of my leadership is supported by the knowledge base about how human beings act, react, and interact? How much is based on my personal preferences and reactions?

- How often are my leadership responses based on habit versus conscious, mindful choice?

- How would the people who observe me as a leader answer the above questions?

- Do I actively work to find out how employees perceive me as a leader? What methods do I use? How open am I to the feedback I receive? How effectively do I use it to grow as a leader?

Capturing the Human Spirit: Motivation and Beyond

Leadership is a 100% human undertaking. The systems leaders create are populated by people, the policies they develop are embraced or rejected by people, the plans they formulate are enacted or ignored by people. Effective leadership, therefore, hinges on a leader's ability to access the talent, enhance the capacity, and develop the potential of human beings. The humanity underlying business and leadership also means that a leader's objective in any task, no matter how routine or mundane, must center on capturing the human spirit.

All of us know that truly great organizations are never built by workers merely following orders or seeking perks. W. Edwards Deming indicated that excellence is 100% voluntary, and deep down we all know why. We know from our own experience, if nothing else, that obedience can produce results, but people's best will never be given without their heart, imagination, and spirit.

> *Leadership is a 100% human undertaking. Effective leadership, therefore, hinges on a leader's ability to access the talent, enhance the capacity, and develop the potential of human beings.*

Obedience can produce results, but people's best will never be given without engaging their heart, imagination, and spirit.

To make strides in this direction, leaders must first understand the raw materials they have to work with, the people they oversee. Human reality, at its most basic, has both a physical aspect and a non-tangible or spiritual aspect.

These two elements underlie the many experiences – work history, family life, hobbies, opinions, skills, possessions – that shape each of us as unique individuals. They also provide the foundation on which we function in a professional capacity.

As leaders, we tend to focus almost exclusively on the professional performance of our employees. We fixate on this aspect and often give little thought to the humanity on which it rests. In many ways this mindset is understandable. One-dimensional, task-related abstractions like "welders" or "programmers" are much easier to supervise than flesh-and-blood human beings with shaky marriages, sick kids, and unrealized aspirations. Yet the idea that employees – or leaders – check their humanity at the workplace door is a fiction as preposterous as it is counterproductive. Leaders might fancy the idea of single-purpose "workers," but human beings are what they will always get. As Anita Roddick, founder of the second largest cosmetics franchise in the world, said, "We were looking for employees, and people showed up."

The only way to tap into voluntary excellence is for managers to create environments in which the whole person thrives and grows. Leaders must base choices on the principles of the human knowledge base and must use their authority to create a culture that takes into account the total human being upon which professional performance lies. They must create conditions that motivate people, not "employees," and that engage the human spirit.

What Motivates People?

Because it is so closely entwined with capturing the human spirit, the issue of motivation deserves further exploration. What stimulates sustainable motivation? What can leaders do to leverage the power of fundamental values? How can leaders move beyond the superficial motivation of extrinsic rewards?

These are questions that were considered by Frederick Herzberg, one of the foremost authorities on workplace motivation. Over several decades of research Herzberg explored the issue of motivation through in-depth, open-ended interviews. In these interviews he asked employees at every level to describe times when they had been truly satisfied by their work, times they had been personally committed, eager to get to the job, and willing to go the extra mile, not because it was expected but because they wanted to. He collected their accounts, analyzed them, and identified common or recurring themes.

The results of his efforts were enlightening. Out of the vast range of factors that could motivate a person in the workplace, Herzberg found that a relatively small number were mentioned again and again. The following factors were among those most frequently described by the employees he interviewed:

1. **Achievement.** More than any other factor, employees indicated that the chance to achieve something personally meaningful was a source of significant motivation.

2. **Recognition.** Human beings are social creatures, and the opinion of others exerts a strong influence on our outlook and disposition. Having our work recognized by supervisors and even coworkers and customers therefore provides a strong source of motivation.

3. **Work itself.** Herzberg's findings were published at a time when many leaders felt that employees needed to be coerced or bribed into doing work. His research found that work itself – the creativity of designing advertisements, the thrill of committing high-stakes financial transactions, the personal connection of caring for patients – is a powerful source of motivation.

4. **Responsibility.** Increased organizational responsibility provides motivation in several ways. Typically it brings duties that are more strategic, substantive, and challenging. But increased responsibility also sends a powerful signal that we are respected and valued enough to take on tasks of importance.

5. **Growth and development.** Few experiences provide more satisfaction than exercising one's natural talents. Opportunities to expand and develop capacities, then, offer a natural source of motivation.

These findings are valuable in themselves, but Herzberg's research did not stop there. He also asked employees to describe times they had been particularly dissatisfied, uninterested, and unengaged in their work. This question produced a range of demotivators much like the motivators above. Topping this list were:

1. **Company policies and procedures.** Confusing, unnecessary, or illogical red tape is aggravating in any situation, especially when it prevents us from doing the work expected of us. It is no wonder, then, that employees described policies and procedures as their number one source of demotivation.

2. **Supervision.** Polling has consistently shown that employees quit managers far more often than they quit companies. Poor supervisory practices were the second most frequently mentioned source of demotivation.

3. **Workplace relationships.** We all interact with others in our work, and these interactions exercise great influence over our disposition. Negative relationships, whether intimidating, antagonistic, or frustrating, are a powerful source of demotivation.

4. **Working conditions.** Workplace conditions are a classic source of discontent. Whether physical danger, onerous working hours, or inadequate equipment, adverse conditions are a perennial source of demotivation.

5. **Salary.** Though salary is widely considered the fundamental reason people work, money only gets people in the door. It does not capture their spirit. The size of a paycheck can demotivate employees, but receiving a raise produces no additional work being done.

One of the strongest messages emerging from Herzberg's research was that true motivation is not something that can be given by someone from the outside, but rather must come from within each of us. A sense of achievement in work well done, the satisfaction of increasing responsibility, the pleasure of doing an enjoyed task – none of the most common sources of motivation identified by Herzberg can be given by leaders to employees directly, like a raise or a benefit package. Leaders can create the conditions in which motivation flourishes, but they never create motivation directly. Put simply, leaders never motivate employees; they create cultures and environments in which employees' inherent motivation manifests itself.

Put simply, leaders never motivate employees; they create cultures and environments in which employees' inherent motivation manifests itself.

What does this mean? It means that people want to work. We want to contribute to meaningful goals, we want to be placed in environments in which our capacities are fully utilized. This intrinsic human drive lies at the heart of the comment that excellence is 100% voluntary. Leaders will rarely if ever be able to "motivate" employees to excellence. What they will be able to do, however, is create conditions in which employees voluntarily give their all to a project or goal they believe in. If they view their employees as unwilling partners in need of motivation, leaders will always be "pushing the rope" toward excellence. With an understanding of the basic human desire for meaningful endeavor, leaders will face the far more exciting prospect of unleashing and harnessing the human spirit already filling their workplace.

Motivation, Demotivation, and Leadership Choices

Motivation and demotivation might seem like two sides of the same coin, but Herzberg's research revealed that they are less intertwined than one might guess. Rather than being opposing ends of the same spectrum, it turned out that they operate on two different scales altogether. The research clarified that motivation and demotivation are influenced by different factors and therefore, the level of one does not necessarily predict or determine the level of the other. Because of this lack of direct linkage, human beings can be both motivated and demotivated at the same time. We can be excited by the responsibility of a new job while being discouraged by the red tape involved. We can enjoy the recognition of heading up a high profile project while chafing at the restrictive supervision of our boss.

The capacity to be simultaneously motivated and demotivated holds important implications for leaders. Demotivators are what cause employees to grumble, what cause them to quit their jobs or form unions, and therefore occupy the majority of leaders' time and attention. But even if a leader could create ideal policies and perfect workplace conditions, he would not have increased motivation. Employees might not be discouraged, but neither would they be motivated. New policies, pay packages, and parking lots can remove sources of irritation, but they cannot capture the human spirit. This is important for leaders to understand because removing negatives, although important, achieves only a state of neutrality, not the excellence to which leaders aspire.

The knowledge base outlined by Herzberg presents leaders with an important point of reflection: how are you choosing to allocate your leadership time between supplying motivation and removing demotivation? Are you contenting yourself with simply addressing grievances? Or are you actively working to grab your employees' imagination and fire their interest? Your department need not be curing cancer to capture the spirit of employees. Motivation can be fostered in any industry and at any level of responsibility, provided leaders are working to do so and consciously reflecting on their efforts. Although leaders inevitably face conditions beyond their control that disturb employees, they can always provide meaningful sources of motivation. They might not be able to remove the negatives, but they can always make the positives available.

Below-the-Line Inhibitors to Capturing the Human Spirit

Further aspects of motivation will be explored more fully in the following chapters. Before that, however, it is important to consider why Herzberg's research, which has been around for decades, has not more widely influenced prevailing leadership practices.

The answer lies in stubbornly persistent mental models about employees and their role in the workplace. Deeply entrenched in the psyche of leaders and the structure of organizations is the belief that human beings are not and will not be intrinsically motivated, that they are fundamentally averse to work and need to be externally prodded into doing it. This widespread below-the-line belief produces a range of behaviors that strip employees of their fundamental humanity and treat them much like load-bearing animals. To advance projects from stage to stage, to move plans from point A to point B, leaders aim employees in the proper direction and "motivate" them with a swift kick in the rear end. This ubiquitous strategy Herzberg colorfully referred to as "KITA" (kick in the ass) management.

KITA is an undeniably direct way to achieve results. The use or threat of formal or informal reprimands, reductions in pay, reductions of job duties or privileges, and even termination produces immediate, observable action. (Reward-centered systems such as profit sharing and merit-based pay are KITA as well – the carrot rather than the stick, but KITA nonetheless.) The catch is that while KITA management can ensure rote compliance, it will never achieve anything more. It will never create engagement, ownership, or enthusiasm. Moreover, its use undercuts its own efforts. Numerous are the leaders who bemoan the lack of initiative and motivation in employees while creating the very conditions that lead to those shortcomings.

The supposition that employees must be compelled or coerced into work not only contradicts observable evidence, it results in counterproductive actions. A friend of ours is an avid and life-long gardener, the type of person who, if working as a landscaper, would need only the slightest direction to transform a property into a small corner of paradise. But suppose you, as her supervisor, decided she needed to be "managed." Suppose you gave her a single tulip bulb and said, "Take this outside and plant it where the X is marked on the ground. I will come by later to check your work. If it's satisfactory, I'll give you another bulb to work on." And further suppose that company policy required her to secure written permission to pull any weeds under two inches tall and file a requisition order to use any company spades or rakes. What would her attitude toward gardening be then? Would she wake up excited about doing work that she loves? Or would she dread another day at the grindstone?

Intrinsic motivation is the heart of productivity and commitment, but such motivation can easily be negated by workplace culture. Hiring the right people for the job is important, but it will never be sufficient to guarantee superior organizational performance, because organizations are constantly hiring the "right" people –

people well-suited to their positions and capable of making significant contributions – and promptly turning them into the "wrong" people.

> *Organizations are constantly hiring the "right" people – people well-suited to their positions and capable of making significant contributions – and promptly turning them into the "wrong" people.*

In the circumstances of the example above, our gardening friend would unquestionably be a terrible employee, filled with resentment, hostility, or indifference. She would not only *seem* like a bad-attitude employee, she would actually *be* one. But while a supervisor would rightly identify her as a problem employee, that supervisor would be mistaken in assuming that she walked in the door that way. She was the world's most enthusiastic gardener when she was hired, and it was only through her supervisor's choices, both in direct supervision and in formulating policies, that her attitude soured.

This example is clearly exaggerated, but it illustrates the way we leaders perpetuate systems that deny or overlook fundamental sources of human motivation every day. We create or allow conditions that demotivate employees without ever realizing it, and just as importantly, we fail to supply conditions leading to meaningful sources of motivation. We reduce the significance and meaning of workplace endeavor to the lowest common denominator, and as a result, countless employees who love the work they do become needlessly negative about their jobs.

Are *You* Capturing the Human Spirit?

Many employees are cynical, apathetic, disillusioned with their work. This is a sad truth of the workplace. What is also true, though, is that none of us *want* to feel that way about our work. We would all rather be motivated than unmotivated, would all rather be fired up about the work we do than indifferent. Given that human beings have a fundamental desire to be engaged at the level of the spirit, the question leaders must ask themselves, then, is not *Why aren't these employees engaged?* but *What elements of my workplace culture are preventing them from being engaged?*

KITA-tinged leadership can be found everywhere. If you are thinking to yourself *but I'm not a tyrant – I'm one of the nice guys,* consider the following. Leaders may praise employees' accomplishments, ask after their families, and remember their birthdays, yet believe that employees will not work unless supplied with external reasons to do so. The problem lies in the below-the-line mental models that are held. Do *you* as a leader believe that human beings are intrinsically self-motivated or that people must be bribed or coerced into doing work? This question is far more than an abstract consideration, for KITA patterns of thought produce KITA-based cultures, which in turn produce employees who are obedient but only marginally engaged.

Research-based know-ledge about human beings is not new, and few of its principles are

Research-based knowledge about human beings is not new. Rather than seeking different answers, we would be far better served by holding the mirror up to our beliefs and considering how closely they match the knowledge base.

particularly surprising or revolutionary. Just as diet and health studies regularly emphasize a few well-known ideas – eat more fruits and vegetables, get more exercise – the findings about the health of human interactions have been remarkably consistent. Rather than seeking new answers, then, it seems we would be far better served by holding the mirror up to our beliefs and considering how closely they match the knowledge base of proven and dependable principles.

Reflecting on what you truly believe – your theories-in-use, not just your espoused theories – is imperative in capturing the human spirit. Research has shown that motivation, engagement, and enthusiasm stem from a relatively limited number of sources. But only to the extent that you believe achievement, recognition, responsibility, development, and the act of work itself will truly engage employees, will you choose to supply those elements in a meaningful way. And only to the extent that you see them not just as being important, but critical, will you tap the human potential of those around you.

Think again of the kinds of questions Douglas McGregor posed. Do you believe that the average human being can find work a source of satisfaction? That most employees have the capacity to exercise a relatively high degree of imagination, ingenuity, and creativity in the solution of organizational problems? That even frontline employees seek a sense of meaning and accomplishment in their work? Your views on such below-the-line issues determine the culture you are building for your employees, and therefore demand your constant reflection.

Questions to Ponder – Capturing the Human Spirit

- What do I believe causes employees to be motivated?

- What do I believe is my role in employee motivation? What leads me to believe this? Where do my beliefs about motivation come from, and upon what are they based?

- To what degree do I, as a leader, operate as if human beings are intrinsically self-motivated? To what degree do I operate as if people must be externally enticed or coerced into doing work?

- In what ways am I creating conditions that lead to employee motivation?

- What am I doing that might undermine employee motivation? What conditions have I created or allowed that may diminish employee motivation?

- How much do I rely on KITA-style management techniques to get people to work? How would my employees answer this question?

Vision: The Emotional Connection

A client once took us on a tour of an 800-person plant manufacturing transmissions for 18-wheel tractor-trailers. The facility's machinery was awe-inspiringly complex, but the plant manager's remarks focused on a newly adopted manufacturing process and the documentation it required. Seeing a worker filling out some of this paperwork, the manager asked the man why he thought these charts and graphs were necessary. The man spoke of ensuring quality and efficiency, to which the manager agreed, but said there was more to it than that.

"The reason we track these statistics," he said, "the *real* reason we do all this stuff is that someday some trucker is going to be tearing through the panhandle of Texas at 2:30 in the morning, trying his best to make a delivery on time. He's going to be tired and alone, and whether he knows it or not, he will be trusting us to give him a transmission that won't break down. He'll be depending on us for his livelihood and safety, and we can't let him down. He's the reason we fill out these forms every day – because it's our duty to take care of him and everyone like him."

Though some might view these words as little more than a rousing pep talk, the plant manager was in fact doing something of great importance: investing an otherwise mundane task with significance. He was reframing an employee's view of the purpose of his work by placing a routine duty within a context of *meaning*.

We human beings seek meaning in life. We seek it in our personal lives, our family lives, and our hobbies. Research has also amply demonstrated that we seek meaning in our work life as well. We want to further something larger than ourselves, and if given the chance, we will work committedly to advance endeavors we see as being of significance.

Unfortunately, meaning is often in short supply in the workplace. Leaders are well skilled in directing the work of employees but far less adept at articulating why that work matters.

> *We human beings seek meaning. Unfortunately, meaning is often in short supply in the workplace. Leaders are well skilled in directing the work of employees but far less adept at articulating why that work matters.*

Why does an organization offer the products and services it does? What need is it filling? What is it contributing to the world? Even if leaders give thought to these questions, their conclusions rarely reach the employees clocking in and out every day.

Questions of meaning make little difference to leaders who hold a strictly external view of motivation. Employees will still follow directions with no sense of purpose in their work. They will still lift what they are told to lift and file what they are told to file. But rarely will they go beyond that, rarely will they spontaneously give of themselves in the way that so often makes the difference between mediocrity and excellence. As Warren Bennis wrote, "Without meaning, labor is time stolen from us." Leaders that hope to create a workforce filled with investment, motivation, and ownership have no choice but to find ways to suffuse their workplace with meaning.

Making Meaningful Achievement Possible

As detailed in the last chapter, achievement was the factor most often cited by employees in Herzberg's research as a source of significant motivation. But while working toward and achieving goals is indisputably inspiring, the goals we pursue must be understandable and meaningful to capture our interest and enthusiasm. To motivate us, the ends we work toward must be embedded in a larger context of purpose and contribution. They must, in other words, be part of a meaningful vision of the future.

Perhaps you have heard the parable of the three bricklayers. Coming across three masons hard at work on the side of the road, a traveler asks each what he is doing. The first remains at his work and says simply, "Laying brick." The second looks up and replies, "Constructing a wall." The third wipes his brow and says, "Building a cathedral."

The moral of the story, of course, centers on vision. Vision is that essential bond that connects the duties we are asked to perform with the aims those duties advance. Vision tells us where we are going and invests our work with meaning and significance. Fired by a clear and compelling vision of the future, the intern no longer makes copies simply be-

A compelling vision of the future is what makes meaningful achievement possible.

cause he is low man on the totem pole. Instead, he is providing a service, however mundane, that facilitates the distribution of resources to those in need. Motivated by a meaningful sense of mission, the receptionist answers phones not just to earn a paycheck, but to further the production of a product beneficial to the public. "A shared vision is not an idea," said Peter Senge in his seminal book, *The Fifth Discipline*. "It is not even an important idea such as freedom. It is, rather, a force in people's hearts, a force of impressive power." Vision is what raises a job to a calling. It is the difference between a workman laying brick and a workman building a cathedral.

A compelling vision of the future is what makes meaningful achievement possible. Consider again the work of the three masons. The first lays a brick, lays another, lays a third. He can churn out plenty of product, but he can *achieve* almost nothing because his work, in his eyes, is nothing more than an endless string of bricks. The second enjoys a much greater capacity for achievement because of his wider scope of purpose. He can admire the craftsmanship of the walls he has built, can appreciate the attention to detail that his efforts showcase. But only the third has an emotionally resonant concept of his work. He can take pride in finishing the sanctuary where the faithful will pray, can feel satisfaction in setting out the courtyard where children will gather, can appreciate the effect of the ornamentation that will greet travel-weary pilgrims. He can know, at the end of a long day, that he has accomplished something of value.

Achievement requires a standard by which success and failure will be judged, a definition of what is actually being accomplished. Vision provides this standard. Vision

Vision does not change the work that is done, but it does change the context in which that work is pursued. It changes how work feels as nothing else can, and without it the concept of achievement is a pale and empty abstraction.

does not change the work that is done – the masons are all using the same bricks, the workmen are all building the same truck transmissions – but it does change the context in which that work is pursued. It changes how work *feels* as nothing else can, and without it the concept of achievement is a pale and empty abstraction.

Leadership Implications

The human knowledge base is becoming increasingly clear about the role of vision in the workplace. Vision is an indispensable part of organizational culture that impacts everything from involvement to ownership to motivation. But what does this mean in terms of leadership choices? What decisions should leaders be making in light of this knowledge?

The concept of vision presents leaders with at least three arenas of choice: having vision, communicating vision, and living vision.

Having Vision

It is not uncommon to hear people speak about creating or crafting an organizational vision. These terms are not inaccurate, but they misconstrue a central and critical reality: that true vision is less *created* than it is *excavated from within*. Vision is something all of us have already, something that needs to be found rather than created, articulated rather than crafted. For some leaders vision lies near the surface and is readily accessible. For others it must be found though a sustained process of inquiry and discovery. By looking within for vision, leaders find not only what will inspire themselves, but what will resonate with others.

What goes into a compelling vision? Marketplace metrics have a role to play, but vision cannot be entirely or even predominantly defined by them. Similarly, money is indispensable to organizational functioning, but research has shown that the pursuit of profit will never create enthusiasm and commitment. Employees do not cherish dreams of market share in their hearts, and dedication will never be summoned by the prospect of happy shareholders or smiling board members. To capture the spirit of employees, daily tasks and goals must be made meaningful on a human level. People must be galvanized by a vision of meaningful service.

To provide this vision, leaders need to ask themselves not only why their organization and its products and services *do* exist, but why they *should* exist. To pull the best from their employees, they need to answer who really cares if their business exists at all and why humanity is better off with it than without it. Vision, at its highest, defines an organization by societal contribution. In the end, vision is leaders' articulation of an organization's best contributions and their personal dream of its most inspiring future.

Communicating Vision

Once a leader has articulated to himself the vision he has found within, that vision must be shared. A vibrant and meaningful vision starts with leadership but cannot remain there, for vision is effective only to the extent that it is communicated and collectively owned throughout an organization. As Frederick Smith, founder and CEO of FedEx, once said, "The primary task of leadership is to communicate the vision and the values of an organization."

A vibrant and meaningful vision starts with leadership, but vision is effective only to the extent that it is communicated and collectively owned throughout an organization.

We once had the pleasure of visiting a well-known family resort famous not only for its spotless grounds, but for its ability to maintain that standard of cleanliness using teenager employees whose mothers cannot get them to clean their rooms. Seeing one such teenager patrolling a plaza with a broom, we introduced ourselves and asked him to tell us about his job. The young man described the kinds of duties one would expect, but when we asked what he was trying to achieve with his work, he, knowingly or unknowingly, began describing a powerful vision of service.

"Everybody who comes here has problems," he said. "They have problems when they come, and they'll have problems when they go. What we try to do is create a fantasy world where, for at least a little while, they can forget their problems." Impressed by the answer, we asked how he furthered such a noble goal. He shrugged and said, "Sweeping junk off the ground."

What is important to realize is that the attitude of this young man was no accident. It was the effect of a leader-created culture that surrounded even mundane tasks with meaning. And because it was a systematic element of culture, that attitude proliferated throughout the organization, regardless of the individual employees filling given positions.

To establish vision as an element of culture, it must be communicated throughout an organization not just once nor even periodically, but constantly and continuously. It must be not only an object of communication itself, but the context in which all other communication takes place. Though some leaders appreciate the importance of communicating vision, almost all drastically underrate the work needed to establish vision as an element of workplace culture. In his *Harvard Business Review* article "Leading Change: Why Transformation Effort Fail," John Kotter, author and professor, suggested that most organizations undercommunicate their vision by *a factor of ten.* Consider the scope of that discrepancy: for every time the average leader refers to an organizational vision, Kotter says he or she should do it nine times more.

Living Vision

Vision must go beyond talk if it is to consistently shape workplace dynamics. It must be put it into practice. Expanding on this theme, Kotter said that leaders must incorporate vision into their hour-by-hour activities to the degree that they become "a living symbol of the new corporate culture." They must drive their vision of a preferred future down to the lowest levels of an organization, for only if it is meaningful to the frontline employees who produce the products and interact with the customers will it have an appreciable impact. To influence the behavior of clients and customers, vision must matter to those who work at the most nitty-gritty levels.

This will not happen through a vision statement alone. Organizational vision is an animating ideal shared by people working together toward a common goal. Organizational vision statements are an administrative tool. Vision statements can be an effective means to communicate organizational goals and aims, but they can also be hollow pieces of bureaucracy. The value of a vision statement, then, lies not in its mere existence, not in the fact that an organization has created and distributed one, but rather

> *In order for vision statements to be meaningful and relevant, leaders must continuously be breathing life into them through their actions, attitudes, and decisions.*

in the impact that vision has on how people think, feel, and behave.

In order for vision statements to be meaningful and relevant, leaders must continuously be breathing life into them through their actions, attitudes, and decisions. To do this leaders must consistently connect the vision to the decisions they make, the conversations they hold, the coaching they do. They must clearly operationalize it in organizational policies and procedures. They must connect the dots between the tasks employees accomplish and the vision those tasks further. Because without such leadership attention and action, a vision statement is nothing more than a piece of paper on the wall.

What does an organization with an exemplary sense of vision look like? Our consulting experience has shown that truly vision-driven organizations weave purpose so thoroughly into daily operations that it is never far from the surface. Employees in such organizations sense the vision behind the tasks they do, and not only can they speak about that vision with eloquence and precision (both in general terms and in regard to their particular position), they are eager to do so. They are excited about what their organization does and what it stands for and because of this excitement, leaders do not have to wonder whether or not their people "get" the vision. It is something they talk about all the time.

Of crucial importance, then, is the degree to which you are personally vision-driven in your work. Your vision must be communicated to employees not only formally but in the many subtle ways that mark it as a true operational priority. Though vision might mean the world to you, if all your employees see you focusing on is filling beds or trimming costs, they will give

> *Of crucial importance is the degree to which you are personally vision-driven in your work.*

little credence to what you *say* about the vision. Only if they perceive your daily interactions as being guided by a consistent and compelling vision will that vision resonate with them as well. And only to the extent that your employees see a vision genuinely reflected in your actions will that vision take root.

Job Description Versus Vision

Most employees, if asked about their job, will describe the tasks they perform. "I keep the president's calendar and make her travel arrangements," they might say, or "I oversee maintenance and repair of the company's network servers." If you press further, though, and ask what they are trying to *achieve* by those tasks, many will hesitate or stumble, because many have little sense of the larger goals they are working toward.

> *Only to the extent that your employees see a vision genuinely reflected in your actions will that vision take root.*

Moreover, a distressing number will indicate they are just trying to get from one day to the next, saying things like, "I'm trying to stay out of trouble, that's what I'm trying to achieve."

In the absence of a compelling vision of the future, organizational functioning tends to become calcified and highly dependent on formal job descriptions. People perform tasks not to accomplish goals or aims, but simply to discharge the responsibilities of their position. The office manager orders supplies not to assist in providing better service to clients, but because that is what the office manager does. The department head holds weekly meetings not to inspire or direct the team he oversees, but because that is what a department head does.

In addition, over-reliance on job descriptions blocks employees from any meaningful sense of achievement and ownership. Job descriptions are, of course, a necessary tool. But unless they are supported by an animating vision of the future, an organization will never reach its potential, despite even furious levels of activity. Only when leaders place job descriptions within the context of a compelling vision can organizational excellence be created and sustained.

It is important to note that the work of an industry does not, in itself, provide vision. Healthcare facilities and social service agencies provide unquestionably commendable services, but the cultures within such organizations can be as mechanical and job-description-oriented as any shop or manufacturing plant. Vision is never self-evident; the energy and attention of leaders is always required to supply it.

What does this mean to you as a leader? Putting it directly, if job descriptions are standing in for vision in your organization, it means that, in all likelihood, your theory-in-use is that all people really need to do their job well is clarity about tasks. It also indicates a belief that people basically have no interest in, or need for, a greater context that gives those tasks meaning. To infuse your employees' jobs with meaning and significance, to truly open the door of achievement to them, requires that you fill their workplace with a pervasive and animating sense of vision, mission, and purpose. This will not just be a matter of changing your behavior; it will require the discipline of reframing your understanding and beliefs about the essence of true human motivation.

Reflecting on Vision

Employees can bring many things to the office, but workplace vision is not one of them. Remember the plant manager who described so eloquently why producing quality truck transmissions was important? Two years before that episode, he had come to the plant as its new manager. He drove the new manufacturing process into the plant with rigid displays of top-down authority. He offered no real ownership of the process to his employees and therefore faced a long and uphill battle. His top-level managers voiced support only because it was politically expedient to do so. His shop employees used his "fancy" system only resentfully and avoided it whenever possible. And though a few realized the potential of the new process, most awaited the day that the new manager would go away and everything would return to normal.

The story could have ended in disaster, but happily it did not. As time wore on, the manager began honestly considering his employees' views of himself, his leadership style, and his plans for the plant. He began reassessing his entire approach to leadership. After some very difficult introspection, he began articulating the passion he had had all along. In doing so he instilled a far deeper purpose and meaning in the process he was introducing and thereby created a compelling vision for his employees to embrace. Where his fervor had previously been expressed through KITA-based pressure (because he believed that was the only way to get people to change), he now began expressing his passion in ways that advanced the changes he was introducing. And as he more mindfully modeled the vision and values he espoused, he won the commitment and energies of employees from frontline staff to senior management.

The benefits of vision are clear; the critical role it plays in the workplace is evident. As always, though, the important issue is how you as a leader think about vision. What is your below-the-line understanding of vision and its role in the workplace? What day to day choices do you make with that understanding? And how do others perceive the choices you are making? Your vigilant reflection on these questions is key to making your organization committed, enthusiastic, and vision-driven.

Questions to Ponder – Vision

- What is my below-the-line thinking about the role of vision in organizational functioning? Do my leadership actions seem to indicate that I believe that employees can find opportunities for meaningful achievement without an understanding of the big picture surrounding their jobs?

- Do I have a compelling vision for the future of my organization? What is that vision?

- How consistently, and in what ways, does my vision impact my decisions, focus, actions, and use of time? How clearly do I think my employees see this vision reflected in my leadership choices and actions?

- How clearly would my employees be able to say what my vision is? To what degree do they understand it? To what degree do they have a collective sense of ownership of it?

- In what ways have I made vision a core element of my organization's culture? In what ways do we use the vision to determine actions, make decisions, formulate plans, and solve problems in our organization?

- To what degree does this vision create a context in which work is done and evaluated? In what ways do I explicitly connect employee's accomplishments with the achievement of the vision?

Recognition: Acknowledging People's Worth

6

In their best-selling book, *First, Break All the Rules,* Marcus Buckingham and Curt Coffman had over 80,000 managers in some 400 companies interviewed to identify characteristics common to high-performing organizations. Thousands of questions were asked, refined, and discarded until only twelve remained, representing the "core elements needed to attract, focus, and keep the most talented employees." Among these twelve – among the top four, in fact – was this simple question: *In the last seven days, have I received recognition or praise for doing good work?*

It should come as little surprise that recognition was identified as one of the foremost determinants of a strong and successful workplace. After all, recognition was the second most frequently mentioned source of motivation in Herzberg's research. But this confluence of research only validates what we already know from personal experience. We can remember how we have felt when our work was praised by an appreciative supervisor. We know how quickly our outlook can improve when the boss sincerely thanks us for the grunt work we do month in and month out. We understand how recognition can inspire us to exert greater efforts and strive for greater achievements.

The human knowledge base could not be clearer in this regard, and yet recognition is sadly lacking in the workplace. Though recognition represents a free, immediately implementable, and constantly available source of motivation, employees from top to bottom say they wish they received more appreciation for the work they do. Everyone from executives to fry cooks say that while they frequently hear about mistakes they have made, only rarely are

> *Though recognition represents a free, immediately implementable, and constantly available source of motivation, employees at every level say they wish they received more appreciation for the work they do.*

they told they have done a good job. Such is the scope of this challenge that in our twenty five years of consulting work, we have encountered only seven departments in which employees felt they were genuinely and sufficiently recognized.

We once worked with the leadership of a steel foundry in eastern Pennsylvania. The foreman of the facility told us that when he was first hired, he received performance reviews on all employees on a regular basis. Flipping through them one day, he noticed that one long-time employee named Joe had been doing particularly good work the past several weeks. Wanting to recognize and encourage such performance, the foreman called Joe over the next time he saw him. He said he had noticed the quality of Joe's work and wanted to thank him for everything he was doing for the organization.

In recounting the story in our seminar, the foreman noted that Joe stood well over six feet tall and weighed upwards of 250 pounds with not an ounce of fat on him. He was a hard man through and through and not someone looking for charity from anyone, the foreman told us. But as Joe stood in the heat of the foundry floor that day, tears began to stream down his face. "I'm sorry," he said to the foreman, obviously embarrassed. "It's just that I've worked here for seventeen years, and this is the first time anyone has ever thanked me for something I've done."

That the contributions of countless human beings – foundry workers, waitresses, managers, vice-presidents – go unrecognized for weeks or even years at a time is simply a fact of life. Whether you feel this is morally acceptable or not, another fact of life is that workplace conditions such as these are not without bottom line consequences. Joes across the nation do their jobs, and many do them well, but their full potential is squandered day after day, for people will never exert themselves *fully* for the sake of a leader or organization that takes their efforts for granted. They might do what they are asked, but rarely will they offer the kind of personal effort and commitment that builds truly outstanding organizations. Without sincere recognition, building employee commitment and initiative is effectively impossible.

Appreciation: The Heart of Recognition

To truly recognize the contributions of employees, leaders must attend to three interrelated areas. They must:

- Have a true appreciation for employees and their efforts

- Communicate that appreciation to employees

- Ensure that their appreciation is conveyed in a form and with a frequency that is perceived to be meaningful by employees

Considering the first point, the knowledge base is clear: we human beings want to be appreciated and valued in the work we do. Recognition, though, is only as good as the spirit that animates it. Because recognition is a fundamentally above-the-line behavior, it can be disingenuous as easily as it can be sincere, perfunctory as easily as heartfelt. Recognition, as an above-the-line action, must therefore be rooted in appreciation, as a below-the-line quality of spirit, if it is to be meaningful to employees.

Leaders who wish to more effectively recognize employees must begin by taking a candid and penetrating look at the fundamental beliefs and outlooks shaping their behavior. Do I have a sincere and personal appreciation for the contribution of employees? Do I genuinely feel gratitude for the work employees do? Do I have a truly appreciative heart? The answers to these questions will go a long way in determining the impact of efforts at recognition.

Appreciation is critical to effective leadership. In our consulting work we have gone so far as to tell leaders that if they do not sincerely appreciate their employees, they should get out of the business of leadership. We say this not to be harsh or condemnatory, but simply in acknowledgment of the fact that recognition is far too important to be marginalized or trivialized. Re-

> *Recognition is only as good as the spirit that animates it. If leaders do not sincerely appreciate their employees, they should get out of the business of leadership.*

cognition may focus on the work being done – the project being furthered or the goal being pursued – but to the recipient, recognition is invariably personal. Plans and projects might be what people talk about, but *we* are the ones doing a good job, *we* are the ones contributing to a program, *we* are the ones being thanked and valued. Recognition concerns people, not tasks. And because it is such a personal issue, no one will be satisfied with a boss who does not value efforts and recognize contributions. Moreover, no human being will feel he or she deserves to work for a supervisor who does not value his or her efforts.

Communication and Perceptions of Recognition

Having appreciation for the contributions of employees is a first step, but that appreciation must then be communicated to individuals, teams, and departments in personal and meaningful ways. This is no small challenge and requires leaders to establish recognition as an operating priority.

Efforts to communicate recognition are inevitably hampered by the effects of perceptions. We human beings are acutely aware when our efforts go unrecognized – *I worked all weekend on that report and she couldn't even manage a lousy 'thank you!'* – but we are almost unable to realize when the labor of others has gone similarly unacknowledged. Often we will not know an employee worked all weekend preparing the report, and even if we do, it simply will not mean as much as if it had been *our* free time spent on company business. Our own labors will always be more real to us than those of our employees, and because of that, we will rarely give as much recognition as we would expect and hope to receive for the same amount of work. Time after time we will give less than we would want to receive.

Compounding this challenge is that while recognition is a primary source of motivation, its lack is not often a source of significant complaint. Employees will not grumble, and there might be few overt symptoms. But a lack of recognition and appreciation will steadily eat away at morale and blunt enthusiasm. Put simply, a lack of recognition will not sink the ship, but it will prevent the sails from ever becoming fully filled.

To measure the effect of their efforts, leaders must ascertain how employees view the recognition they receive. Formal surveys and interviews have their place, but leaders must also take time to get to know the people they supervise. Just as generic gifts are never as meaningful as those reflecting a person's individual likes and dislikes, generic recognition will never be as effective as recognition that is infused with an understanding of the person being recognized. They must determine the degree that employees feel they are appreciated, using the employees' perceptions – and not their own – as the standard of their effectiveness.

> *A lack of recognition will not sink the ship, but it will prevent the sails from ever becoming fully filled.*

Appreciating What Employees Do and *Can* Do

We once undertook a survey of employees in a software development firm in Nebraska. We met with a cross section of staff and asked them a number of open-ended questions, one of which was, "How do you know if you are doing a good job?" As is typical of many organizations, most employees said they didn't really know; a few found out only in their annual performance review. In one department, however, employee after employee told us that their department head believed in them even more than they believed in themselves. They said she not only appreciated what they had done, she also continually expressed confidence in their abilities and encouraged them to take on and succeed at new projects. More than a few said that under her leadership they had grown in ways they hadn't known were possible.

When we met this woman, it was immediately clear that she understood the power of encouragement to an unusual degree. She explained that in her view the fundamental role of leadership was "harvesting the talents of people." She took it as her responsibility to look for the strengths of employees, even those still undeveloped, and recognize, encourage, and nurture those strengths.

> *To offer effective recognition leaders must reflect not only on the choices they are making, but on the beliefs that drive and shape those choices.*

The approach she outlined not only sounded good, it got results. The difference between the functioning of her department and most others in the organization was night and day, and it is little wonder why. We all appreciate having our potential acknowledged, and rare is the person who would not be motivated to demonstrate further capacity when warmly encouraged to stretch and take risks. An important question for leaders to reflect on, then, is the degree to which they look beyond what employees have already done to find what they *could* do with appropriate encouragement, mentoring, trust, and support.

Mental Models Inhibiting Recognition

Decisions of how, when, and in what venue to recognize employees are fairly straightforward, but they rest on below-the-line mental models. Unless those foundational paradigms about human nature and the responsibilities of leadership are examined and transformed, they will pull leaders' actions back to what they have always been. To offer effective recognition, leaders must reflect not only on the choices they are making, but on the beliefs that drive and shape those choices.

These beliefs are plagued by a number of misconceptions. Many spring from views of human nature that were common in the past, but have been shown to be incomplete or flatly inaccurate. Among these misconceptions, many of which still exist, are:

- **Not part of a leader's job.** Many leaders conceive of their job in purely operational terms. In their mind, their job is to ensure that patients' needs are dependably tended to, that marketing campaigns are launched on time, that products are produced efficiently and reliably. Lost in this view is the means by which these goals are met, namely, the human side of leadership. If leaders do not see building an effective human system as part of their job description, it goes without saying they will fail to accurately recognize their employees. This KITA-based view inaccurately frames recognition as a perk that is, in the final analysis, unnecessary.

- **Pay is enough.** Some leaders feel that personal appreciation from a leader is simply not necessary. Many feel that the paycheck employees receive is thanks enough, and that any expectation of recognition or appreciation beyond that is unreasonable and unwarranted. These leaders typically hold a mental model that money is the primary reason human beings work.

- **Neediness.** Some leaders question why they should be expected to applaud every little thing employees do. They bristle at the idea of "babying" employees for fulfilling responsibilities that are theirs in the first place. Such objections spring from below-the-line attitudes that frame the need for recognition as a form of immaturity. Research, though, has consistently shown that having one's efforts recognized and validated is a basic psychological need. Refusing or neglecting to provide it does not make organizations and employees stronger, it makes them weaker.

The above misconceptions all incline leaders away from recognizing their employees. Different lines of thinking inhibit leaders who sincerely believe they already give sufficient recognition but in fact do not. These well-meaning leaders are affected by several habits of thought that limit the effectiveness of their recognition. These pitfalls include:

- **Formal recognition policies.** Leaders often institute formal recognition programs. These programs are well intentioned, but all too often degenerate into impersonal expressions of corporate bureaucracy. Scott Adams, creator of the "Dilbert" comic strip, shared this example: "As I approached the front of the room to accept my award, it became apparent that the executive running the program didn't know what I did for a living. Thinking quickly, he invented an entirely fictitious project for the benefit of the audience and thanked me for my valuable contribution to its success." Recognition programs are not inherently bad, but they do amount to corporate policies, and it is important to remember that policies and procedures were one of the top five sources of demotivation identified by Herzberg.

- **Generic compliments.** Adams' story also touches on the issue of specificity. To be meaningful, recognition must be specific, concrete, and informed. It must spring from time spent with employees and familiarity with their capacities and duties. Most of us have had the boss who threw "good job!" around liberally to motivate the team, and we know how hollow such generic compliments can sound. We need only think back to a past supervisor going through the motions to understand why effective recognition must rest on leaders' personal involvement and investment.

- **Above and beyond.** Leaders often associate recognition primarily with outstanding or unusual accomplishment. Out of the ordinary victories should certainly be celebrated, but every organization relies on numerous positions that, while indispensable, offer few opportunities for above-and-beyond distinction. Given that organizational performance can depend in large part on these jobs, leaders must expand their understanding of recognition to include and embrace contribution as well as distinction. Recognition of this kind applauds the unobtrusive, behind-the-scenes kinds of service – the night janitor keeping the hallways spotless for years, the mid-level accountant submitting timely and accurate reports month after month – that can so easily be overlooked or taken for granted.

- **Every couple of months.** Many leaders feel, accurately, that they recognize their employees. What they fail to do is give recognition at a level and frequency that impacts employees' views of themselves, their work, and their organization.

Remember the frequency of recognition mentioned at the beginning of the chapter: whether an employee feels he or she has received recognition or praise in the past seven days. Many of us recognize employees; very few of us aim for that level of frequency and consistency.

Reflective Leadership and Recognition

Recognition is an acknowledgment of the contributions made by others. In a much deeper sense, though, it is an acknowledgment of the value and worth of an individual. We all want to be recognized for what we do, but even more we want to be appreciated for who we are. This is true in regard to our leaders, our friends, our coworkers, and our family. It is a universal human desire.

Recognition and appreciation are issues impacting our fundamental sense of human importance. The questions leaders must ask in regard to them are weighty: What below-the-line beliefs about the human beings I employ are evidenced by my actions? To what extent do I honestly appreciate the work my employees do? How grateful am I for the contributions they make? If, at the level of reflection these questions explore, you realize that you do not truly harbor appreciation for your employees' efforts and contributions, an attitude problem exists that training will not address.

If, however, you realize after serious reflection that you do sincerely value the people you employ, the questions become: How intentionally do I express my appreciation? How clearly do my employees perceive that appreciation?

These questions address not only the act of recognition but the deeper issue of whether you as a leader have a truly appreciative heart. Being sincerely grateful for employees' contributions will right a thousand lapses of leadership technique, while taking them for granted will undermine a thousand otherwise commendable efforts.

Questions to Ponder – Recognition

- What do I believe are a leader's responsibilities in relation to appreciation and recognition? What do my actions in relation to recognition reveal about my thinking about the human beings I employ?

- To what degree do I truly appreciate the human beings working for me? In what ways do I express appreciation for the contribution of employees?

- How much do I rely on formal recognition programs, versus personal and/or informal expressions of recognition?

- What keeps me from expressing recognition and appreciation to employees more than I do? What elements of my below-the-line thinking in relation to recognition may need to change?

- Do my employees feel recognized and appreciated for their good work?

The Art of Involvement 7

The complexity of business today requires a range of talents far exceeding the capacity of any one person. No longer can a leader chart a path to the future based only on his or her own understanding and judgment. On the contrary, success has increasingly come to depend on leaders' ability to gather a diversity of talents and draw from them coherent and actionable strategies. As leaders are thrust into the role of facilitator among experts, the ability to involve employees in collective decision making becomes an essential element of effective leadership.

Such employee involvement is also a key component in capturing the human spirit in the workplace. As employees, we might have a meaningful vision from our leaders. We might even feel adequately recognized by them. But if we are not allowed to take part in the decisions that affect our work, we will not feel a part of the organization. We will do our work, but we will not take owner-ship of it or give our best to it because it will not be ours, but someone else's.

Why, then, are leaders often reluctant to involve employees in day to day affairs? In many cases the reasons leaders prefer to make decisions unilaterally lie with their perceptions of themselves and their employees. We leaders often assume that since we were promoted into leadership, we must be smarter, more creative, better decision-makers, etc. than our employees. We assume that involving those employees would introduce inferior ideas into deliberations and unnecessarily slow the decision-making process.

The human knowledge base, however, indicates just the opposite. Research has shown that involvement is one of the most effective ways of tapping the collective intelligence of an organization. Studies have shown that group decision making is more effective than individual decision making in many kinds of situations. One study (Hall & Williams), for example,

Employee involvement is a key component in capturing the human spirit and tapping the collective intelligence in the workplace. Why, then, are leaders often reluctant to involve employees in day to day affairs?

showed that with basic training in consensus decision making (collaborative leadership, flexible patterns of communication, cooperative problem solving, etc.) a group-crafted solution is superior to the best solution of any individual member of the group some 75% of the time. Put simply, involving employees in the decision-making process will yield better results three times out of four, *even if a leader actually is smarter, more creative, and a more capable decision-maker than her or his employees.*

Group decision making does not "average out" the talents and capacities of individual members, but rather adds (or multiplies) them. Far from detracting from the efficacy of the decision-making process, it generates possibilities that none of the participants would have come to on his or her own. And as leaders become ever more dependent on the specialized and technical knowledge of their employees, involvement will become less a choice than a necessity.

Increased Ownership

Improved decision making is one benefit of involving employees, but not the only one. When human beings are involved in determining a course of action, they come to view that action as their own. Contributing our thoughts and ideas to a project (and perceiving those thoughts to be sincerely received by our leaders), we take ownership in that initiative, feel we have a personal stake in whether it prospers or fails, and do what we can to support it. Conversely, when we are excluded from the deliberative process, we care little whether something succeeds or fails. Sometimes we might even root against initiatives from which we were excluded.

> *When we human beings are excluded from the deliberative process, we care little whether something succeeds or fails.*

We once worked with a fire chief whose budget contained money to buy a new fire truck. The chief was looking through a catalogue one day, trying to decide what equipment to order, when one of his men asked what he was doing. The chief explained the upcoming purchase, and the man immediately called the rest of the station to come take a look. Within moments the chief's small office was crowded with men viewing the catalogue and discussing varying options with great enthusiasm and excitement.

When the truck arrived, it was the pride of the station. The men cleaned it, cared for it, and talked it up to anyone who would listen. The chief's counterparts at the city's three other stations told a different story, however. Their men, they said, roundly disliked their new vehicles and grumbled incessantly about everything that was "wrong" with them. One went so far as to say he sometimes wished he had never bought a new truck.

The chief was surprised by the difference in reaction, but the kicker, he later told us, was that the four vehicles were not only comparable but almost indistinguishable from one another. The equipment and features were nearly identical. But where the chief's men had been involved in the decision-making process, the others had merely been assigned something by a superior who had not bothered to seek their input or opinions (even though they would be the ones driving the truck and using the equipment). That simple act of involvement, the chief said, turned out to be the only difference between employees who were proud and excited and employees who were disgruntled and resentful. In this regard the chief experienced firsthand what research has shown time and again: that the act of involving people in the decision-making process builds ownership of decisions and motivation to support them.

Leaders often say people resist change, but this is not quite true. As a general rule we human beings do not resist change, we resist *being changed*. The ownership that results from involvement is the key difference between the two. When we are involved in the process of change, when we are given some input on its direction and course, we are quite willing

When we are involved in the process of change, when we are given some input on its direction and course, we are quite willing to pursue change.

to pursue change. The firemen in the one station were involved in the change affecting them. The firemen in the others were not, and the difference could not be more stark. With nearly constant change being the reality of business today, involving employees in decisions of all types is not only important but imperative.

The Most Profound Form of Recognition

If recognition is an acknowledgement of the worth of a human being, how can you tell if someone really values you? What demonstrates his or her regard? What are its outward manifestations?

When asked this question in workshops, participants often say things like "they seek me out," "they spend time with me," "they share thoughts and ideas with me," "they ask my opinions," "they listen with real interest." The behaviors they describe shed light on a fundamental truth of human interaction: involvement is perhaps the most profound form of recognition one human being can give another. You can applaud your children's intelligence or maturity, but if you do not involve them in decisions affecting the family – buying a new house, moving to a new city – that praise rings hollow.

Involvement may be the most profound form of recognition one human being can give another.

You can tell your wife you love her, but if you never seek her thoughts or opinions, she will not feel valued. Involvement is one of the clearest and most immediate ways to acknowledge the worth of another human being.

Expressing appreciation for efforts and thanking people for the work they do is extremely important. But words alone can only go so far. Sharing information, discussing ideas, or soliciting input demonstrates regard in a way that few other leadership actions can. It communicates an appreciation for talents and contributions by actions, and not just words alone. It shows that you value people's capacity to think, not just their capacity to work.

Leadership Implications of Involvement

The human knowledge base details numerous benefits gained from involving employees in daily decisions and organizational issues. "Participative decision processes…can provide a training ground in which people can think through the implications of decisions," wrote Victor Vroom, a researcher who explored employee involvement for decades. "Participation can also perform a team building function, building positive relationships among group members and helping meld them into a team. Finally, participation can aid in aligning the individual goals of group members with the goals of the organization."

Leaders who want employees who can think through the implications of their decisions, who can work effectively as a team and align themselves with organizational goals, need to involve their people in the decision-making process. Those leaders need to seek employees out, ask their opinion, and give focused attention to what they have to say. These things can be done formally or informally, in group settings or one-on-one dialogue, but the more complex the problem to be solved, the more important it is to involve others.

In a previous chapter we noted that the internal quality of a workplace is strongly

Organizations in which employees feel their opinions matter are organizations in which morale is high, confidence is palpable, and efforts are unified and mutually reinforcing.

correlated to the degree that employees feel their supervisors use organizational authority for them as opposed to on them. A similar indicator is the degree that employees feel leadership values their thoughts and ideas to the point that leaders *consistently seek out* and *actively listen to* those views. Organizations in which employees feel their opinions matter to leaders are frequently organizations in which morale is high, confidence is palpable, and efforts are unified and mutually reinforcing.

It is important to note that involvement as we are using it here does not necessarily imply democracy. It does not give employees the final say, nor does it obligate managers to implement all employee suggestions. What it does imply is an honest consideration of employees' thinking and a regard for the legitimacy of their judgment. Like so much else, involvement depends almost entirely on leaders' below-the-line beliefs and attitudes. When all is said and done, the degree to which you value the thinking and judgment of others is what matters. Going through the motions of soliciting input when the outcome of the decision has all but been made is an empty show that will do more harm than good.

> *Involvement's effectiveness rests entirely on the degree to which a leader truly values the thinking and judgment of others.*

Below-the-Line Obstacles to Involvement

Given the benefits to be gained in improved decision making, increased ownership, and meaningful recognition, why don't leaders involve people as much as they can? In helping clients uncover below-the-line obstacles to involvement, we have observed a range of factors.

Among these are the hierarchical systems of authority that characterize virtually every modern organization. These hierarchies, which impact all leaders to one degree or another, contribute to mindsets that tend to create unfounded assumptions about who has capacity and who does not, who is a decision-maker and who is not, who is qualified and who is not. These dichotomies are widespread in the workplace, but leaders who subscribe to them unwittingly overlook vast reservoirs of talent, creativity, expertise, and imagination.

Leaders' personal views of themselves and their relationship with employees can also present serious obstacles to involvement. Among the more common beliefs that need reexamination are:

- **The belief that it is the boss's job to make the best decision.** Many leaders believe that making the best decisions possible is a central element of their position. This view is not incorrect, but a more complete and accurate mental model is that it is the boss's responsibility to ensure that the *best decision is made.* Though initially it may seem little more than a minor nuance of meaning, this distinction is very important, for research has consistently shown that involving others leads to more effective, creative, and accepted decisions.

- **The belief that seeking employee input takes too much time.** Perhaps the most common objection to involvement is time. It is true that involving employees does require an initial investment of time. What is also true, however, is that involvement is almost always more efficient in the long run. When making a decision unilaterally, a leader's first task is invariably selling that decision to employees to gain commitment and support. A decision involving employees from the beginning, however, already enjoys, by virtue of the participative process, the support and buy-in of those needed to see it to completion. It creates a team already optimized to succeed in its task.

- **The belief that an open door policy is an adequate channel for soliciting input.** Many leaders have a genuinely open door, but even the most sincere open door policy puts the onus of communication on the employee. Involvement is not a passive affair, not a matter of being *willing* to listen if an employee has a concern or idea. True involvement stems from a leader's conviction that involving employees in decision-making processes is for his or her benefit as much as employees themselves. It means proactively and consistently seeking employee input on matters of importance.

We once presented a group of client leaders with the following question: *What is preventing you from applying the knowledge base related to involvement?* The group had been working on this area for some time and was consequently able to engage in this self-analysis with a frank and fearless degree of honesty. Some additional below-the-line dynamics they uncovered were:

- Fear of surrendering authority and control
- Fear of losing importance
- Fear of being upstaged or outperformed by employees
- Fear of appearing unknowledgeable or incompetent
- Lack of trust in employees and coworkers

- Fear of exposing inconsistencies or deficiencies in personal thinking or decision making
- Lack of a positive relationship with those who would be involved
- Preferring to seek input from those who already agree with our thinking

If these issues seem exceptionally personal, the clients themselves were surprised at how many obstacles rested on their own fears and insecurities. Owning up to such fears required a stout commitment to hanging the mirror, and their willingness to acknowledge personal challenges is an example worthy of emulation. Only when such issues are first identified and then addressed can progress be made. Short of this no tactical tinkering will produce meaningful involvement.

What Leaders Value

We leaders fail to fully involve our employees in workplace decision making for a variety of reasons. Some of the most common were described above, but they may have even deeper, more profound roots. The issue underlying nearly all failures of involvement can be found in two fundamental below-the-line attitudes:

- Not valuing the thinking of others

- Not believing that other people's thinking can enhance our own

These inhibitors are about as fundamental as beliefs come, addressing bedrock views of worth and contribution. Might either of these ways of thinking apply to you? Before you answer, consider the task of moving a piano. If you were called to move a piano, you wouldn't hesitate to ask for help. Your physical limitations would be clear, and you would simply ask several friends to lend a hand. When we make leadership decisions, though, we often rely only on our own views and expertise. Because the need for help in decision making is more subtle, we feel we can go it alone, but on this point the human knowledge base is clear: regardless of how we view our abilities and those of the people we supervise, we will make consistently better decisions by involving others in our thinking and deliberations.

Consistently better decisions are made by involving others in our thinking and deliberations. Yet, the hard reality is that many of us do not really value the thinking of others and do not believe that it can improve our own.

The hard reality is that many of us do not really value the thinking of others and do not believe that it can improve our own. This is not a conscious theory that we espouse, but rather one that is revealed by the leadership choices we make. We say we believe others' thoughts can enhance our leadership, and indeed we truly do believe it at the level of abstraction. Yet when it comes time to reorganize the department or open the new site location, we just don't feel that this is the right situation to start involving employees. We believe in involvement, just not today.

Reflecting on Involvement

Involvement is a straightforward concept that can escape even the best leaders. "Collaboration is at the heart of successful decision making, but somehow this fact eludes us," wrote Peter Grazier, consultant, trainer, and author on employee involvement and empowerment, in his article *What Is Team Building Really?* "Teaming isn't something we do because it creates harmonious work groups, or is neat to do. It is a way to formalize the power of collaboration among individuals. It is a way to blend the talents, skills, and inherent creativity of diverse people. It is a way to use this collaboration so that the work group leverages its skills, time, and resources for their own benefit and that of the organization."

The piece Grazier wrote chronicled his transition from a stand-alone decision maker to an inclusive leader, a journey that began with a simple experiment. "Simply think of some decision you need to make, then ask someone for their thoughts. If you want to really expand the possibilities, get several people together and ask them to discuss the issue. Then take notes. When you are alone, look at your notes and see how many new facts and ideas have been added."

Grazier's inquiry was born out of personal initiative, but it took on added significance when he was asked to lead several new problem-solving groups in his company, groups that "were given some of the most difficult problems the organization faced. They were problems whose solutions had eluded both management and the hired experts for several years.

"We assembled these teams, comprised of 'ordinary' people from the workforce, and began to dissect the issues and brainstorm solutions," he wrote. "Solutions always emerged. A phrase I came to use a lot to describe these solutions was 'brilliant simplicity.' I was always surprised, at least at first, by how people with diverse knowledge, talents, and skills were able to combine these qualities to arrive at a place that was greater than any of them could have individually."

Central to Grazier's experience is what we would term a below-the-line change in thinking and outlook. "Although I was observing this phenomenon almost daily in my work, it took almost four years before my own decision making process became more naturally collaborative. As I have looked back on my own transition, I have gained a greater awareness and appreciation of the difficulty of changing ourselves, let alone others. My prior conditioning prepared me for a world of individual accomplishment and competition, and so I never acquired collaborative skills. It took a series of significant emotional events (i.e., collaborative workplace breakthroughs) to have me seriously reconsider how to contemplate, explore, and make decisions differently."

Notable in Grazier's account is the determination and consistency of effort needed to produce lasting change. It took him four years to truly recast his below-the-line attitudes about participation and involvement, a victory won through no small amount of exertion. This effort is to be expected, for improvement comes not by turning away from challenges but by grappling with them head-on. Leaders improve by hanging the mirror and asking tough questions: Do I have genuine respect for the skills and abilities of my employees? Do I believe that my thinking and decision making will be improved through their contributions? Do I define my job as making the best decision or ensuring that the best decision is made?

Questions like these pose a clear challenge to every reflective leader. In the end, the degree you involve your employees depends on your confidence in the human capacity around you and the extent to which you view employees as legitimate partners in planning and problem solving. Only by hanging the mirror and taking a good look at how you view the human beings around you can you create an environment of involvement that fosters truly excellent performance.

Only by looking first at yourself can you hope to adequately involve others.

Questions to Ponder – Involvement

- Do I believe that employee thinking is important to effectively solving organizational problems, making better decisions, and improving my own thinking? How clearly do I put that belief into practice on a daily basis?

- How much do employee opinions matter to me? Do I genuinely value the thinking of my employees to the point that I actively seek it out?

- Why don't I ask for employee input more than I do? How open am I to considering that my thinking may need to change? In what ways may my thinking need to change?

- How much do I experience fears related to involvement such as surrendering authority and control, losing importance, being upstaged or outperformed by employees (and others listed on pp. 92 and 93)?

- In what ways am I creating conditions that lead to employees having a sense of ownership in their work? What am I doing that might undermine employee ownership?

- How would my employees answer the above questions?

Communication: Making Things Common

8

Anytime two or more people pursue objectives in tandem, they create a human system. The quality of this system's functioning depends first on the mindsets that shape its participants' actions. Second only to that is the communication on which the system relies. Communication is the means by which understanding can be built. It is how diverse talents can be directed toward a common goal, and an array of individual *I's* can be transformed into a cohesive and capable *we*. It is what makes coherent collective action possible.

Much of this book has revolved around communication in one way or another. Building culture, expressing values, articulating visions, and conveying appreciation all rely on the ability to communicate with others. But despite its importance, communication is an area of struggle for almost all organizations. The concept has been stressed, exhorted, and invoked so frequently that its meaning has been all but lost. "Good communication" has become to the workplace what "playing nice" is to the schoolyard – an idea that is commendable in concept but largely undefined in practice.

Effective patterns of communication rest on countless daily interactions, but communication is, fundamentally, a *human* endeavor that involves much more than the surface-level transmission of facts and information. No matter how large organizations might grow, no matter how remote and removed parties might seem from each other, communication is always a matter of one human being connecting with another.

Building Connections of Relationship

Communication is the method we use to make things common. Linguistically related to the words "common," "communion," and "community," communication is the means by which we offer private thoughts, beliefs, and perceptions. It is how we make what is internal available for external consideration, discussion, and action. It is the way we share of ourselves and have access to the experience of others.

Though we do it almost continuously, communication is more personal than many realize. Communication allows us to express ourselves and gather information, but it also builds the connections that lead to relationship. It draws individuals and groups together into a shared community of thought and discussion, if only for the duration of a conversation. This community-building function is of great importance, for only to the degree that leaders are willing to enter into "communion" with employees will they be able to establish effective workplace communication. If leaders hold themselves above or apart from employees, communication will inevitably falter, for leaders will be denying the fundamental underpinnings on which it is based. Communication, then, depends as much on what leaders believe or don't believe about their

> *No matter how large organizations might grow, communication is always a matter of one human being connecting with another.*

employees as it does on what they say or don't say. It depends as much on values, beliefs, and attitudes as it does on structures, systems, and approaches.

Content Communication

Communication can be divided into two broad categories: content and relational. Content is the *what* of any message. It is the facts and figures, ideas and opinions that we transmit through an e-mail, conversation, memo, or note on the bulletin board. It is anything that can be expressed in words.

Organizations in which facts and information are available, accessible, widely dispersed, and understandable can be said to have communication-rich environments. These environments nurture effective human systems in which employees are enabled to take ownership, make independent decisions, further organizational goals, and work effectively in teams. In contrast, environments that lack this breadth and depth of communication lead to workplaces characterized by confusion, isolation, misunderstanding, lack of unified effort, and duplication of effort. Employees in such organizations understandably tend to lack initiative and ownership of their work.

Communication-rich environments create conditions in which employees can take ownership, make independent decisions, further organizational goals, and work effectively in teams.

Most leaders recognize that organizations with vibrant and plentiful communication function far more effectively than those with poor or merely adequate communication. What leaders often fail to realize, though, is that such conditions do not come about by chance. Communication-rich cultures are established through conscious effort and consistent reflection on the part of leadership. Such environments are built as surely as warehouses and factories, and require every bit as much effort and attention.

To create communication-rich environments, leaders must elevate communication to an organizational priority and make it the object of attention and measurement. They must also model openness and genuine inclusiveness, and demonstrate the behaviors they wish to see in others. Asking for a free flow of communication from employees while neglecting to provide it *to* them creates a double standard that undermines leaders' efforts.

> *Communication-rich environments are built as surely as warehouses and factories, and require every bit as much effort and attention.*

Breaking Content Communication Down

When leaders assess communication in their organizations, they often speak in terms such as "good communication" or "communication problems." Such expressions are natural but obscure a great variety of context and circumstance. To better understand the variety of workplace communication, it can be helpful to think in terms of topic-specific categories of communication. Identifying these content areas allows organizations to more accurately assess exactly how and where communications succeed and falter. One organization, for example, might excel at communicating policies but struggle with training and skill development. Another might communicate goals and objectives effectively but stumble in conveying organizational vision and mission.

In our workshops we sometimes ask participants what types of content communication they and others would need to do their jobs effectively. The answers they give describe categories of communication that can be found in most organizations. Among these are:

- Vision and mission
- Goals and objectives
- Job descriptions
- Policies and procedures
- Standards and expectations
- Organizational relationships and structures
- Feedback
- Decisions and the rationale behind them
- Training and orientation
- Available resources
- Deadlines and priorities
- Plans and changes
- Hot issues
- Market conditions

Once leaders identify the categories of content communication within their organizations – by first posing the above questions to themselves and then posing them to employees – they can begin gauging the effectiveness of specific areas of communication. Often they find communication is strongest in concrete but prosaic areas like policies, procedures, and job descriptions. More abstract but substantive areas like vision, mission, and big-picture goals are often communicated much less effectively.

Decisions are a weak area of communication in many organizations. The *who's*, *what's*, and *where's* of decisions are communicated with relative reliability, but in our experience the rationale, the *why*, behind them often is not. Employees are given the operational outlines of upcoming changes – this project is being cut, this department is being reorganized – but the reasons necessitating those changes remain a mystery. This partial communication ensures that employees can follow the narrow instructions they are given but are powerless to go beyond *this* task or *this* job. Because of the lack of rationale, they are unable to help leadership achieve the goals underlying specific instructions. For example, a leader might ask employees to remove a lamp from a table, but unless employees are told why – the room is being redecorated and the lamp is the wrong shade of yellow, the desk needs to be dusted, more light is needed in another part of the room – they cannot undertake other initiatives that would further leadership's ultimate aim, like removing the yellow potted plant as well, getting the duster out of the closet, or turning on an overhead light. They can do nothing but wait for their next instruction.

As a leader, then, you can have enormous impact on your organization just by communicating reasons as widely as you communicate decisions. In so doing, you will also build trust, provide employees with a more sophisticated understanding of complex issues, and heighten problem-solving capacities throughout the system.

Feedback – information on the results of employee efforts – is another area prone to inadequate communication. Employees often say they are given very little information about the outcomes of the work they complete. They may be told they have done exceptionally well or poorly, but rarely are they told what impact their work is having on larger organizational objectives like reducing departmental expenditures or raising levels of customer satisfaction.

This lack of feedback hinders employee development and inhibits ownership and involvement. To understand why, imagine going bowling and having a curtain dropped across the alley every time you stepped up to throw the ball, preventing you from ever seeing how many pins you've knocked down. Consider how many times you would be interested in throwing a ball with no information on the results of your efforts, and you will quickly

> *Lack of feedback hinders employee development and inhibits ownership and involvement.*

understand why feedback is central to fostering employee engagement. By giving clear, concrete, and constructive feedback on the results of employee initiatives, you can ensure that they don't feel like their efforts disappear into a black hole.

Conversation: Shared Frames of Reference

As organizations grow, they become increasingly reliant on memos, newsletters, and speeches. But as seemingly efficient as these forms of one-directional communication are, they can convey only a limited degree of complexity, nuance, and detail. Leaders might, for example, inform employees that the company is heading in a new direction. Yet the many subtle implications – the structures that will be needed, the priorities that will shift, the impact on organizational culture – will never be established through email blasts alone. To clarify these finer details of content, two-way communication is needed, and that means conversation. Conversation is the indispensable means of building shared layers of understanding. It is the way complex ideas take on life and depth at all levels of an organization.

> *Conversation creates a self-correcting loop that leads to greater degrees of shared understanding.*

Conversation establishes a mechanism for refining meaning and intent. The ask-listen-discuss cycle of conversation creates a self-correcting loop that inevitably leads to greater degrees of shared understanding, regardless of the communication skills of the participants involved. In our consulting work we have frequently demonstrated this clarifying function through the use of a simple but eye-opening exercise.

The exercise has two phases. In each phase one member of the group is designated as the leader and the others as employees. The leader is given a diagram of seven geometric shapes and told that his job is to describe that arrangement in such a way that the employees can duplicate it without seeing it. In the first round the leader is told not to take any questions from the group members, and the group is told not to ask any. They are simply to do their "job description" and follow the directions they are given. In the second round a new designated leader is told to solicit questions, listen carefully, and generally try to ascertain the degree of understanding and comfort of the group members. Similarly, the group is told that not only can they ask questions of the leader, they should not let the process move forward until they fully understand what they are supposed to do.

The results of the two phases of the exercise are as different as night and day. In the first, regardless of how explicitly the instructions are given, it is not uncommon for some participants to simply give up out of frustration, thereby becoming recalcitrant "problem employees." Of those who do finish the activity, the accuracy of the drawings varies widely. Occasionally a participant is able to duplicate the leader's arrangement exactly, but this is rare, and the majority do not. Interestingly, the level of confidence is also wide-ranging and largely unrelated to the accuracy of the outcome. Some people are extremely confident but totally incorrect. Those whose work is exactly or nearly right don't necessarily have confidence in their results. In contrast, confidence is uniformly higher in the second round, with most, if not all, participants getting the drawing exactly right. Moreover, the mood of the room is more upbeat, lively, and collaborative. It is not uncommon for applause to break out when the desired arrangement is finally revealed.

This exercise demonstrates the power of two-way communication – conversation – to clarify directions. In real life problem situations, leaders and supervisors often say, "I told them that" or "It's in the manual." This is true, but it misses the point that simply "telling them" without establishing an environment that not only allows but expects questions is an inadequate system of communication.

An added benefit of two-way communication is that it ensures participants are all talking about the same things in the same way. Picture a CEO giving a speech about dogs. While the CEO is envisioning the bulk of a Saint Bernard, some employees are picturing the delicacy of a toy poodle, and one guy, way at the back, is imagining a foot long hot dog with all the toppings. Everyone is using the same terminology, but nevertheless talking at cross-purposes.

Countless misunderstandings result from this type of scenario. Moreover, because people's assumptions are largely invisible – none of us thinks to question what seems obvious to us – such differences can be exceedingly difficult to identify. The CEO assumes everyone is talking about Saint Bernards because it's self-evident to him. The poodle people are equally assured of their view. And the hot dog guy never thinks to confirm that Hebrew Nationals are the topic of discussion, because *that's what everybody has been talking about for an hour.* Or so it seems to him.

Cartoon-like as this example is, the dynamics it presents are serious indeed. How numerous are the fine distinctions of meaning in "team work" or "quality"? How many the understandings of "open communication," "customer service"? This becomes especially important as leaders aspire to establish vision throughout their workplace. They may know exactly what they mean, but they have no guarantee that employees will share that understanding. Only ongoing conversation can clarify meaning and harmonize underlying mental models. Conversation is what allows shared frames of reference to be built among different parties, whether a few office staff or an organization of hundreds.

> *Conversation is what allows shared frames of reference to be built among different parties, whether a few office staff or an organization of hundreds.*

Relational Communication

Everyone understands the importance of content communication and what can happen when it falters: "they never told me," "the memo was confusing," "they let us know too late," "the numbers were wrong." Far more frequently overlooked is the relational aspect of communication. Although we may be unaware of it, content communication is always surrounded by a field of *relational communication* that speaks to the way parties view and are viewed by each other – in other words, the nature of the relationship between them. Our every interaction transmits both surface-level messages (content communication) and the degree to which we respect, value, and consider others worthwhile (relational communication). With every phone call, memo, and conversation, we answer the question "how do you see and value me?" And over time these relational messages become as clear as any email or memo.

Relational messages are not explicit, but they carry great weight. If a coworker invited everyone in your department but you to a social gathering, the missing information of date, time, and address – the content communication – would not be what upset you. If that were the case, you could simply ask a colleague or read someone else's invitation. The problem, rather, lies in the relational communication being sent by your coworker. His or her apparent choice to single you out for exclusion makes an unmistakable statement about the status of your shared relationship.

Three points about relational communication bear particular emphasis:

- **Relational communication is a direct reflection of below-the-line attitudes**. Because we do not intentionally shape relational communication, such messages spring, unfiltered, from our thinking. In other words, our relational communication provides a direct window into our below-the-line attitudes, values and beliefs

- **We are communicating relationally 100% of the time**. Content communication is largely a matter of conscious choice: we make a phone call or we don't, we send an email or we don't. Relational communication, however, is not a matter of choice. We are constantly broadcasting relational messages whether we realize it or not. This means that our beliefs and values, as well as our biases and prejudices, are always leaking out to one degree or another.

- **Relational messages are more important to us**. Because relational messages are linked to how we are valued, our perception of what is being communicated relationally is always more important to us, as human beings, than content or information. When the two conflict, we will always give the relational message (the brusque tone, the clenched jaw) more weight than the content message ("no, I'm not upset").

The implication of these three points is challenging: formal workplace communication is focused almost entirely on content, but every encounter, no matter how dry or mundane, impacts personal relationships as well. How we ask for a phone number, how we hold ourselves as we wait for it to be found, how we take leave of the employee who gave it to us – all send relational messages that have tangible effects on the workplace. The way we interact with and treat our employees impacts how

> *The way we interact with and treat our employees impacts how willingly they collaborate with us, how freely they share information, how likely they are to offer possible solutions, and how effectively their skills can be mobilized to advance the organization.*

willingly they collaborate with us, how freely they share information, how likely they are to offer possible solutions, and how effectively their skills can be mobilized to advance the organization. Outstanding organizations, then, are distinguished by their relational communication as much as by their content communication.

Content communication is easy to track and analyze throughout an organization. Relational communication is much more nebulous because the relational messages each of us are sending are almost invisible to us. Reflecting on these messages, therefore, requires not only a remarkable degree of mindfulness and self-observation, but also a willingness to ask others to help us see ourselves as they do. Creating productive human systems hinges not on camouflaging relational messages we wish to hide, but on spotting and addressing the below-the-line beliefs and values that drive those messages.

To understand the pervasive influence of relational communication in the workplace, put yourself in the shoes of a woman working for men convinced that a woman's role in business ends at answering telephones and serving coffee. Those attitudes would never be communicated formally, of course, would never appear in the employee handbook or mission statement. But wouldn't the point still get across? Wouldn't that woman have a pretty good idea of the lay of the land? The women attending our workshops invariably say they would. They say they would know through the jobs they were given or not given, the information that was shared or withheld, the meetings they were invited to or excluded from, the greeting they received or didn't receive in the hallway.

Do we really think women are as capable as men? Do we really think hourly workers are as trustworthy as salaried ones? Do we really think subordinates have suggestions as valuable as department heads?

These are the kinds of questions that are inevitably answered via relational messages, whether we like it or not.

Dignity and Worth

Relational communication is powerful precisely because it provides a window into what people *really* think of one another as human beings. All beliefs and biases are eventually revealed by relational communication, but perhaps none are as important as those concerning personal dignity and worth. These non-negotiable aspects of self-identity address an individual's role and place in the world. They speak, in a very real way, to our right to exist. Because they are so fundamental, people will never willingly work with someone who does not honor their basic dignity and worth as a human being. You need look no further than yourself to confirm the paramount importance of dignity and worth. How constructively would you work for a supervisor who humiliated and belittled you, who viewed you as expendable or replaceable, or who saw you not as a person but as a tool? Rare, indeed, is the person who would not be ground down by such treatment.

> *Relational communication is powerful precisely because it reveals what people really think of one another as human beings.*

The question, then, is what do the relational messages you are sending out day after day say about your deepest views of your employees? While true tyrants do exist, far more common are leaders who inadvertently and accidentally diminish the dignity and worth of their employees. These leaders are not bad people, but through the habits of KITA-based attitudes, the weight of organizational culture, or just the never-ending press of work, they falter in this most critical aspect of leadership.

We often ask participants where they think protecting dignity and validating worth falls on management's list of priorities. "Pretty low," is the response of many. Even more frequent, though, is the feeling that dignity and worth don't even make the list. This assertion is a sharp indictment of leadership. Organizations can and do function without regard for the humanity of their employees, but the problems they face – low morale, minimal quality, mediocre service, substantial turnover – are as predictable

If employees' fundamental humanity is not respected, they will give little to their organization – and their leaders have no right to expect more.

as they are avoidable. Economic necessity might compel employees to stay in such a workplace, but if their fundamental humanity is not respected, they will give little to their organization – and their leaders have no right to expect more.

Listening

Discussions of relational communication often focus on the negative, dwelling on the potential harm of biases and prejudices (racial, departmental, professional, cultural, etc.) Relational communication, however, has almost unlimited potential for good as well. And listening is probably the most powerful form of relational communication. It is also one of the most profound ways of honoring the dignity and worth of others.

All of us listen. From morning to night we listen to spouses, kids, clients, friends, coworkers, and employees. But the very fact that we do it so much fools us into believing that we do it *well*. The reality, of course, is that our superficial and often scattered attention is no more listening than communication is simply telling people stuff. Listening of this kind is a rough approximation, but little more.

> *The very fact that we listen from morning to night fools us into believing that we do it well. To truly listen, we must genuinely value the thinking of those around us. We must respect them and believe that their thoughts are worth our time and attention.*

Like so many leadership behaviors, effective listening begins below the line in the internal world of attitudes and beliefs. To truly listen, we must genuinely value the thinking of those around us. We must respect them and believe that their thoughts are worth our time and attention. True listening also requires an unequivocal acknowledgement that we don't already have all the answers we need, along with a conviction that our thinking can be enhanced by others' input.

Listening of this kind is as profound as it is rare. Celebrated semanticist and well-known author S.I. Hayakawa describes the difference between this listening and what most of us are accustomed to:

Living in a competitive culture, most of us are most of the time chiefly concerned with getting our own views across, and we tend to find other people's speeches a tedious interruption of the flow of our own ideas. Hence it is necessary to emphasize that listening does not mean simply maintaining a polite silence while you are rehearsing in your mind the speech you are going to make the next time you can grab a conversational opening. Nor does listening mean waiting alertly for the flaws in the other person's argument so that later you can mow him or her down. Listening means trying to see the problem the way the speaker sees it.... Listening requires entering actively and imaginatively into the other person's situation and trying to understand a frame of reference different than your own.

In this light listening is less a skill or behavior than it is a mastery of our own self-centered tendencies. Listening in the way described by Hayakawa requires us to set aside the concerns of our own ego, shelve our personal aims and priorities, sincerely try to understand another person's point of view, and enter into their frame of reference. It means going past what they are *saying* to search for what they are *meaning*. It is, above all else, an act of will. In this sense it is no hyperbole to suggest that human beings can live for years without ever really listening to another person at all.

> *Listening is less a skill or behavior than it is a mastery of our own self-centered tendencies. The problem is not that we don't know how to listen well, but rather that we might not really want to.*

We human beings may have a passing interest in what others say, but as Hayakawa noted, our primary objective is often expressing our own thoughts. It becomes clear that the problem is not that we don't know how to listen well, but rather that we might not really want to. The above quote prompts a series of important questions:

- How often am I chiefly concerned with getting my own views across? *In order to influence, you have to be open to be influenced. To open up to the views of others. To listen, to understand.*

- How often do I find other people's comments a tedious interruption of the flow of my own ideas?

- How often do I simply maintain a polite silence while I rehearse in my mind what I am going to say when I can grab a conversational opening?

- How often do I wait alertly for the flaws in the other people's arguments so that later I can mow them down?

- How often do I try to see the problem the way the speaker sees it?

- How often do I genuinely try to understand a frame of reference different than my own?

Throughout this book we have suggested that the key to effective leadership is reflecting on the process of leadership itself. The questions suggested by Hayakawa's comments present an excellent standard for such reflection. These questions concern the relatively narrow topic of listening, yet in reality their scope is far broader, for they address fundamental issues of who we are as individuals and how we relate to others.

Below-the-Line Inhibitors of Productive Communication

The knowledge base is clear: to build a superior-functioning organization, it is essential to have a communication-rich environment, a culture that protects people's dignity and worth, and an atmosphere in which people feel listened to. Unfortunately, some mental models work against leaders' best efforts to establish productive patterns of communication. Among these are:

- An assumption that one is already communicating sufficiently, along with the related failure to establish systems to validate that belief

- A need-to-know mentality

- A belief that thoroughly communicating with employees is too time consuming

- An attitude equating information with power, and a related fear of losing power by sharing information

- A conviction that employees are not capable of understanding further information

These attitudes, all of which run counter to the observed workings of effective human systems, constitute an important area of leadership reflection and consideration. What and how leaders communicate is important, but even more crucial are the below-the-line values that shape those habits. Leaders whose beliefs are aligned with the human knowledge base will find appropriate and effective channels of communication as a matter of course. They and their employees will find the patterns of communication that work best for their circumstances, and misunderstandings can be corrected by the two-way dialogue of conversation. If leaders' beliefs are not aligned with the principles of that knowledge base, however, no reporting structures or delivery systems will produce lasting improvement. Only when leaders embrace the human-to-human nature of communication will they establish the kind of culture in which employees thrive and excel.

Reflecting on Communication

"In no other area have intelligent men and women worked harder or with greater dedication than ... on improving communications in our organizations. Yet communications has proved as elusive as the Unicorn."

These words are as true today as they were in 1973 when Peter Drucker, considered by many to be the "Father of Modern Management," first wrote them. Communication is an area in which many organizations struggle and even more fall short. But is this difficulty inherent in communication itself or merely indicative of the way leaders approach it?

As noted in the beginning of the chapter, communication is the act of making things common, nothing more and nothing less. It involves making facts and ideas common among employees and then building a community of thought and action around those elements. At its heart, communication is simply the process of expanding understanding to larger and larger groups of people.

Building this shared understanding requires competence in several areas of communication. In order to build an effective community of endeavor, you must share information and data, must issue clear instructions, field questions, and gather feedback through the two-way dynamic of ongoing conversation. You must also attend to the relational aspects of communication, carefully listening to employees, protecting their sense of dignity and worth, and giving consideration to the messages sent by your actions. You must consciously direct all of the messages you are sending, whether formal or informal, verbal or nonverbal, content or relational.

Despite this apparent complexity, we leaders must bear in mind that the underlying reality of all communication is building understanding between human beings. Your reflection on communication must address methods and systems, but it must then transcend such mechanical issues. At its core, communication is one person sharing himself or herself with others, and the quality of your interactions will depend on who you are and how you view others. Hanging the communication mirror as a leader requires pondering challenging questions like:

> *Ultimately, the quality and effectiveness of your communication will depend on who you are and how you view others.*

- Do I believe that employees are getting all the information they need? How do they see it? Why don't I share more information with them?

- Do I believe that employees are truly concerned about helping this organization? If yes, am I giving them all the information they need?

- Do I want employees to demonstrate independent thinking and judgment? And if so, am I giving them information they need to do it well?

- Do I want employees to understand decisions or just obey them? Do I resent being asked why? Do I think that when people ask questions about a decision, they are questioning the decision?

- To what degree do I believe that other people's dignity is important to the quality of their work? How does my communication with them demonstrate what I believe? How do they see it?

- Do I care what other people think? Do I think they have anything of value to contribute? Does my behavior (including listening) demonstrate that?

- To what degree do I believe that creating a communication-rich environment is a high priority?

Your answers to these types of questions will determine how effectively you communicate with the people on whom the achievement of your vision depends.

Questions to Ponder – Communication

- To what degree am I committed to building a communication-rich environment? What mechanisms and approaches do I use to create that environment? How successful are my efforts?

- Would my employees say they work within a communication-rich environment? Would they say they get all the information they need and would like? Do they feel they get the information in a timely and understandable way?

- How effectively do I communicate information related to specific content areas like vision, goals and objectives, feedback, job descriptions, policies and procedures, standards and expectations, organizational relationships and structures, and others (see p. 103)?

- How would I honestly answer the questions (on pp. 115 and116) inspired by the Hayakawa quote about listening?

- How effectively do I communicate with my employees? Do I rely on one way communication? Do I engage employees in work-related dialogue and conversation?

Questions to Ponder – Communication (continued)

- How important to me are protecting my employees' dignity and acknowledging their worth? How does this show in my daily behavior? Do my employees view me as a person committed to protecting their dignity and worth? Does my thinking need to change in relation to this topic?

- Do I listen to employees with a commitment to understanding frames of reference different than my own? Do my employees view me as an effective listener, committed to understanding what they are saying?

- How would I assessment myself in relation to the communication questions on pp. 119 and 120?

The Discipline of Reflection

Leaders seeking to tread a path of continuous improvement and professional growth must grapple with an abundance of reflective questions. How clearly am I painting a meaningful vision of my organization's work for my employees? How frequently am I seeking out my employees' thoughts and involving them in the issues we face? To what degree does the recognition I offer spring from an honest appreciation of my employees' work? How often do I consider the relational messages sent by my body language and tone of voice? To what extent are my daily choices capturing the spirit of my employees, as opposed to simply directing their behavior?

The labor needed to effect real personal change is prodigious. Talking about improving one's communication or consciously protecting the dignity and worth of employees is easy. Taking the first few steps on such a path is relatively easy as well. But following that course to its conclusion – past the dead ends of others' indifference and the brambles of painful revelations – is something else entirely.

Words can give an approximation of the determination required to adhere to a reflective discipline, but they can only hint at the effort needed to transform the fruits of that reflection into meaningful change. If anything, the example of those who have walked this path provides the best picture of the course such a journey might take. In this regard it is useful to consider the experience of a friend and colleague of ours named Grace.

A Hard Truth

Grace was a thoughtful and reflective leader who had become dissatisfied with certain aspects of her life. She worked diligently on the issues that troubled her but found herself unable to resolve them. Because she believed in the discipline of reflective leadership and had taken its principles to heart, she decided to consult a friend whom she trusted to give honest and constructive feedback.

Over a business dinner on the road one night she explained the situation and asked for his thoughts. The friend's analysis, expressed as kindly as possible, was that Grace was a fundamentally poor listener and that this deficiency was impacting many relationships in her life.

These words cut Grace to the core. She put on a brave face to finish dinner, but back in her hotel room she curled up in bed, deeply dejected. Because her job was heavily involved with communication – she was sometimes even called to present training on effective listening – she felt like a failure and a fraud. How could she pretend to teach others what she couldn't do herself, she asked herself over and over again. She stayed awake late into the night, wrestling with questions that seemed to defy answers and taking stock of herself, her career, and her life.

The First Steps of Transformation

The next morning Grace pulled herself together and steeled her resolve. Far from giving up, she decided that she would work on her listening as she never had before. She would spare no effort in finding a way to turn over a new leaf. She would tell her friend nothing of her goal, and she would consider no progress to have been made until he spontaneously and without prompting noted an improvement in her listening.

When Grace set out on this path, she was confident that attention and effort could bring results within two or three weeks. What she found, though, was that in the first two or three *months* her primary accomplishment was simply realizing that her friend had been absolutely right. She truly was not a very attentive listener, and her first task was simply learning how to face that truth over and over again.

As the weeks passed, Grace realized that if she was to improve her listening, she had to become aware of her choices in interacting with others. To listen well, she realized, she needed to recognize when she could and should be paying attention but was not. In the beginning this was simply not possible. Far from being intimately aware of her ongoing choices, she did not identify missed opportunities until hours or sometimes days had passed. But as she continued to strive for mindfulness, the interval between interaction and reflection steadily decreased. Where before she would not reflect on a morning conversation until late afternoon, she now began analyzing it an hour or two later. Sometimes only a matter of minutes passed before she realized that she had not been listening as carefully she might have. She was still not living in the moment, but she was getting closer.

A Deeper Understanding

As Grace brought increasing awareness to the choices she made, she started taking steps to improve her listening. Her first attempts resulted in what she describes as her "face listening" phase. This was a period in which she began consciously and deliberately employing the active listening techniques she had taught so many others. She maintained eye contact. She nodded as appropriate. She gave feedback as good listeners are encouraged to do. But while these behaviors gave her the appearance of attentive listening, her mind was, more often than not, planning a meal for that evening or formulating a list of tasks to be completed by the day's end. She *looked* like a good listener but was actually anything but.

Eventually Grace realized that her efforts at transformation had so far focused solely on above-the-line behaviors. She had been trying to change the external actions she performed, but so far she had given little thought to the below-the-line values and attitudes that shaped those actions.

When she began looking below the line, she came to several important realizations. First she realized that her own inner world was exceedingly vivid and enthralling to her, and she became convinced that if she were ever to become a truly effective listener, she would have to bring as much interest to the views of other people as she brought to her own thoughts. She also observed that she would much rather tell the same well-worn story to someone who had not heard it before than listen and learn something new. She was, she came to understand, more interested in sharing whatever she had to say, no matter how stale and threadbare, than finding out what others had to say.

In contrast to the short term changes of behavior that characterized her "face listening" time, these below-the-line realizations laid the foundation for long term changes of attitude. Grace worked on developing interest in and learning from others, and she struggled to rein in her tendency of single-mindedly sharing things she already knew. She worked hard on changing not just what she *did* but who she *was*. And when, more than six months after their initial conversation, her friend remarked that she seemed to be listening better, she broke down in tears. It was, she said, one of the proudest accomplishments of her life.

Implications for a Reflective Life

This story is the experience of only one leader in one area of human interaction, but it nevertheless illustrates several dynamics that are common to all efforts at personal transformation. The first is simply the amount of work required to effect lasting change in one's approach to others. It is easy to say we are going to change, easy to make plans and preparations. And because of this ease, many of us, like Grace, would probably think that a few weeks of effort should be enough to get the job done. The reality, of course, is that meaningful transformation is rarely quick or easy, and realistic expectations are essential to success.

> *It is easy to say we are going to change, easy to make plans and preparations. The reality, of course, is that meaningful transformation is rarely quick or easy, and realistic expectations are essential to success.*

Another important aspect of engaging in a reflective discipline is understanding where the work of transformation begins and ends. Identifying areas in need of improvement is an achievement of no small magnitude. Ultimately, though, it is only the first of many steps. Difficult at it was for Grace to be told that she was not the good listener she thought she was, that was only the starting point. The real work was yet to come.

Grace's story also highlights the necessity of taking the perceptions of others into account. Grace might well have never reflected on the quality of her listening if not for the comments of her friend. But more than that, her decision to consider her task unfinished until her efforts were spontaneously recognized by her friend obliged her to dig far deeper than she would have otherwise. She later said that if she had not linked her efforts to his perceptions, she would have probably considered herself "improved" after the first several weeks. She would have assumed the great effort she was exerting was having some sort of effect, and she would not have persevered to the point that others could recognize and comment on her strides.

Pegging the success of transformative efforts to the perceptions of other people can be difficult. Much of the work of reflection and improvement is internal, and people will often not appreciate the degree of effort we exert toward it. But while it can be discouraging to have our heroic efforts go unrecognized, we must remember that what matters is the change that comes out, not the effort that goes in. Grace worked assiduously on her inner world, but only when – several months later – that effort become noticeable in her behavior did others take note. Put simply, the work of reflection is largely internal, but not until it becomes manifested in our daily choices does it impact those around us.

Lasting change is rarely easy to achieve. Few of us relish the idea of admitting to ourselves that we don't really care what people have to say, or that we are not really that interested in helping others, or that we are a fundamentally fault-finding person. The prospect of committing months or years to remedying those conditions – work that will likely go largely unrecognized – holds a similarly limited appeal. But looking back on her experience, Grace describes the episode as a great victory and one of the more meaningful periods of her life. It was a success that left her not only a better leader, but a better parent, colleague, spouse, and friend as well. It was an instance of true growth for her, and for us an example of what can be achieved by committing ourselves to a discipline of sincere and ongoing reflection.

Questions to Ponder – Reflection

- How consciously do I take on the task of growth and self improvement as a leader?

- How does my commitment to leadership growth show itself?

- How often do I reflect on my leadership strengths and shortcomings?

- How do I go about seeking out external perceptions about how effective I am?

Optimizing the System: Defining a Culture

Up to this point all the concepts considered in this book have revolved around you. How you can take on the challenge of holding yourself accountable to knowledge-based standards of exceptional leadership. How you can consciously create organizational culture by paying attention to the way you use your authority. And how you can seek input about the impact of your choices on those you lead. This is the foundation of personal reflective leadership.

> *To build an effective organization, you must not only attend to your own actions but also address how the people you oversee view, value, and treat each other.*

Another aspect of leadership needs to be explored, however, before the full discipline of reflective leadership is understood. This aspect relates to the systemic nature of organizations. To build an effective organization, you must not only attend to your own actions but also address how the people you oversee view, value, and treat each other. Achieving organizational excellence requires taking leadership responsibility not only for the way *you* treat persons A and

B, but also for the way person A treats person B, how person B treats all of his or her coworkers, and so forth. An expanded understanding of leadership therefore includes optimizing the system of human relationships to best achieve the ends an organization exists to serve. This requires expanding the target of your attention beyond your own behaviors to include those of the rest of the human beings comprising the system.

Just as the most effective leader is a reflective leader, the most effective organization is a reflective organization. One of the primary tasks of leadership, then, is forging a reflective organization – one in which leaders and non-leaders alike reflect on personal beliefs and actions in light of serving their organization's fundamental purpose. Three crucially important elements must be in place before this is possible.

- The organization must achieve profound unity around the contribution it hopes to make in the world.

- The organization must collectively define the culture by which it will pursue its vision.

- Leaders must vigorously involve people, both individually and collectively, in the conscious pursuit of both vision and culture building.

This chapter will explore the first two of these essential elements in greater detail, while the next chapter will expand upon third element.

Organizational Unity

As we begin this exploration, let us make the starting point abundantly clear. No human system can be optimized, nor can any organization approach its potential, without a pervasive unity of aim, effort, and principles. Achieving this human unity – the ability to work together as a coherent whole while simultaneously maintaining and celebrating differences and diversity – is a concept that is not often mentioned in the discourse about leadership and management, and yet it is the first and most requisite characteristic of a reflective organization.

> *No human system can be optimized, nor can any organization approach its potential, without a pervasive unity of aim, effort, and principles.*

Organizations succeed or fail as a whole system. An organization can no more succeed on the strength of its most-favored aspects than a car can use a functioning drive shaft and carburetor to make up for a dead alternator and flat tires. Systems whose elements are mismatched, sub-optimized, disconnected, imbalanced, or otherwise disunited will fail to reach their maximum potential, regardless of whether those elements be spark plugs and alternators in the automotive world or coworkers, offices, and departments in the business world.

Unfortunately, low-grade levels of disunity – from turf issues, silos, and politics to competition, conflict, cliques, and outright hostility – are present in virtually all organizations. They are a chronic malady that leaders have accepted, learned to live with, and even learned to ignore. But as overlooked as such disunity may be, its long-term costs – reduced productivity, impaired communication, dampened enthusiasm, and recurrent conflict – are steep indeed. While many leaders may choose to simply put up with a certain degree of organizational disunity, the consequences are not unlike

Costly and largely avoidable levels of low-grade disunity are present in virtually all organizations.

financing one's life with credit cards and never paying off the balance. One can learn to survive the costs and acclimate to the hardships involved, but regardless of how "normal" the situation comes to feel, precious resources are being squandered each and every day.

This loss of potential raises a troubling question: why do leaders accept the significant and largely avoidable cost of disunity? Our years of consulting work have suggested two primary factors.

The first is a fundamental misunderstanding of human nature that springs from a widespread below-the-line belief that disunity is just the way things are. "It's just human nature," our clients have said over and over. "People fight, gossip, clash, and there's nothing you can do about it." Unity, in their minds, just goes against our makeup.

Is this true? Is disunity an inescapable feature of human nature? It's certainly true that disunity is not lacking in the workplace. Yet we have personally seen highly unified organizations in which collaboration, mutual assistance, and commonality of vision are the norm, not the exception. This suggests that disunity is not a law of nature, like gravity, but a choice organizations make. The unity organizations can establish if they make it a priority – a unity in which departments go out of their way to help one another, in which all individuals make a point of placing the concerns of the whole organization before their own, in which the success of one individual, office, or division is celebrated as the success of all – is far more than many organizations even believe is possible.

The second reason disunity often remains unaddressed is the strongly held below-the-line mental model that competition has beneficial effects. Competition is almost universally seen as a powerful motivator and effective way to bring out the best in people. Our faith in it so permeates American culture that we aren't consciously aware that it is an opinion and not a fact. Yet author Alfie Kohn, in *No Contest: The Case Against Competition*, demonstrated by citing numerous studies that, contrary to popular belief, in virtually no area of endeavor does competition lead to improved performance or production. Moreover, Kohn argued that competition, by its very nature, is antithetical to collective aims and initiatives:

> Strip away all the claims in [competition's] behalf that we accept and repeat reflexively. What you have left is the essence of the concept: mutually exclusive goal attainment. One person succeeds only if another does not. From this uncluttered perspective, it seems clear right away that something is drastically wrong with such an arrangement. . . . Competition by its very nature damages relationships. Its nature, remember, is mutually exclusive goal attainment, which means that competitors' interests are inherently opposed. I succeed if you fail, and vice versa . . . so the failure of others is devoutly to be wished.

If employees, departments, or other organizational subdivisions are placed in competition with each other, they are implicitly or, in some cases explicitly, cast as competitors who inherently oppose the other's success. Attempts to harness talents, energies, and ideas in such a system face an uphill battle, if they are not doomed from the start. Competitive frameworks also ignore the reality that people in organizations are inherently interdependent. The success of the system as a whole depends not on any one sphere of activity, but on the interaction of them all.

Competition ignores the reality that people in organizations are inherently interdependent. The success of the system as a whole depends not on any one sphere of activity, but on the interaction of them all.

The Two-Fold Task: Reducing Disunity and Building Unity

To the extent that leaders think about workplace unity at all, they tend to think in terms of fixing what's broken. When asked about unity in their organizations, they speak of a lack of friction and discord or an absence of conflict and disagreement. Focusing on negatives that have been solved or prevented, they only rarely can describe proactive steps being taken to build unity.

The following diagram presents a spectrum that ranges from the worst of the worst to the best of the best in relation to workplace unity. On the left are the many forms of disunity we routinely put up with or ignore, the things most of us address only when they get out of hand, when people are shouting in hallways or departments are refusing to work with one another. To build a culture of profound unity, we must move beyond the mindset that correcting problems is all that is required. Just as peace is more than an end to war, a critical aspect of fostering organizational unity is aiming far beyond a mere lack of disunity, moving toward the practices on the right side of the diagram.

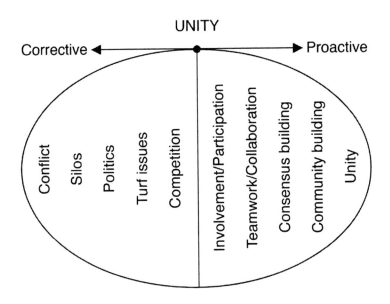

We as leaders must approach organizational unity as both a goal and an operating principle. We must pursue a unified organization through means that are in inherently unifying. We do this by establishing a commonality of purpose, opening opportunities for dialogue, actively involving employees, fostering true teamwork, building consensus, and utilizing collective problem-solving methods.

The critical importance of organizational unity can be difficult to appreciate. So long have the relational credit cards of our organizations been overextended, so often have we heard the refrain "we don't have to like each other to work together" that considerations of unity and disunity can come across as naïve or Pollyannaish. But widespread as these attitudes may be, the fact remains that few issues impact an organization's health and performance more than its level of unity. Any endeavor, big or small, that lacks a dynamic coherence of vision and effort will find itself continuously obliged to expend energy, talent, and resources counteracting the effects of that lack of unity.

Yes, organizations can survive disunity, and yes, the swings of fortune might even endow those organizations with success and acclaim. The mediocrity of their human systems, however, will take its eventual toll. When the crucial patent expires or a well-funded competitor enters the market, the organization will find it lacks the capacity to find its optimal path. Many things can result in temporary success, but only through a profound alignment of aims, values, and aspirations can human systems leverage their internal resources to overcome the next crisis. Any organization can be successful for a time; only unified ones can be consistently great.

Making Culture Shared

Previously in the book we established the importance of both vision and conscious culture building to the personal discipline of reflective leadership. In turning our attention to creating and leading a reflective organization, both of these elements take on additional significance.

Vision not only gives meaning to individual tasks, it lies at the heart of collective excellence. A clear vision – an articulation of why the organization exists and what contribution it seeks to make into the future – is the prime unifying element of any organization, the North Star that everyone within the organization can use to chart a course in alignment with everyone else.

Such vision provides focus for an organization's external efforts, the end results it exists to deliver. Yet essential to accomplishing the organization's *what* – what it is seeking, doing, achieving – is the organization's *how*. How will it pursue its desired outcomes? How will its staff treat each other? How will its people communicate, learn, question? In exceptional organizations the values and principles that guide and shape culture are far from arbitrary or unintended; they are consciously defined and promoted.

A culture's values are the beliefs in which its participants have an emotional investment. Its principles provide a guiding sense of the obligations of right conduct. With no more explanation than this, it is easy to understand the important role they play in unifying organizational functioning. For the people within an organization to come together in a sustained, collaborative, productive effort, then, it is imperative that they have a shared understanding of how they will interrelate.

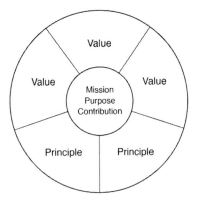

It is, therefore, a leadership imperative to spearhead the process of defining the culture to which they aspire. Pictured here is a simple construct that many of our clients have found useful in articulating the desired culture. Surrounding the vision of its core contribution are the specific values or operating principles to which the organization is committed, explicitly describing the human processes and dynamics by which the organization seeks to make its contribution.

> *For people to come together in a sustained, collaborative, productive effort, it is imperative that they have a mutual commitment to a set of shared values.*

As leaders become increasingly assured that employees know and share the organizational vision and the values animating it, they are confident in giving people wide latitude and freedom. Employees might – indeed, assuredly will – make mistakes. But those mistakes are hiccups arising through honest effort and can therefore be approached as opportunities for reflection, growth, and learning rather than problems requiring correction. Mutual commitment to shared values is instrumental in establishing trust between leaders and employees.

Making a Beginning

Moving from a welter of contrasting below-the-line attitudes to a culture of common aims and shared values is central to optimizing organizational performance, but this does not happen overnight. Research shows that true cultural transformation – changes in values, attitudes, relationships, and principles that become internalized to the point where they are largely self-perpetuating – takes years of leadership focus and effort. Rather than feeling discouraged by this timeframe, rest assured that setting an organization on a path toward a culture change can have an almost immediate impact. New systems will take time to develop, but as leaders consciously reflect on both organizational output and organizational functioning – product *and* process, contribution *and* culture – system performance will improve and the organization will become increasingly effective in achieving its central mission and purpose.

Questions to Ponder – Unity and Cultural Values

- Do I believe that disunity is normal and inevitable in organizations, or that whole-system unity can be achieved if targeted?

- Do I believe that low-grade levels of disunity don't significantly inhibit system functioning or that high levels of unity are required for system optimization?

- Do I consistently work to reduce divisive aspects in our organization? How?

- Am I proactively working to build unity in our organization? How?

- What can I do to reduce competition and increase cooperation in our system?

- Does our organization have a clearly defined set of values? How much are they reflected in the way we operate? How effectively are they communicated and discussed?

- Do I engage in the hard work of incorporating these principles into my daily behaviors? Do I consistently exemplify the cultural values?

- How would my employees answer the above questions?

Optimizing the System: Engaging Other People

As the previous chapter underscored, a shared culture is essential to a unified and cohesive human system. It is the only way a leader can ensure that everyone within the system shares the same vision of the future, supports the same goals, embraces the same priorities, champions the same values, agrees on the same strategies, and adopts the same collective identity. It creates the opportunity for employees to become participants in the construction of their own organizational environment.

However, crafting and articulating an image of the desired culture is only the beginning. By itself, that image is like a blueprint of an office building yet to be built. No matter how expertly drawn the schematic might be, its potential is only latent until people are engaged in the process of building it.

Throughout this book we have suggested leadership success is all about you. The first, most important leadership choice you must make in engaging other people is to personally play an active role. The degree to which people perceive you as a consistent champion of the targeted culture – striving to be an example of its values, engaged in the hard work of translating its principles into daily behaviors, and willing to reflect and hold yourself accountable to its standards – will determine the degree to which they are willing to join your culture building efforts.

> *No speeches you deliver, no matter how eloquent; no posters, no matter how well designed; no statements or slogans, no matter how articulate, will suffice to change culture. If you are not manifestly engaged with the stated values of the culture, no one else will be.*

No speeches you deliver, no matter how eloquent; no posters, no matter how well designed; no statements or slogans, no matter how articulate, will suffice to change culture. People are always watching you as their leader, and if they do not perceive you as sincerely living the culture, the only result will be skepticism, if not cynicism. For this reason your own alignment with the stated values of the culture must be a daily source of reflection. If you are not manifestly engaged, no one else will be.

Beyond your own active involvement, however, there are two other levels of engagement that demand your attention as you strive to optimize the system you lead. The first engages other leaders while the second, ultimately, includes everyone in the organization.

Expanding Your Focus – Engaging Leaders

Many leaders manage not only frontline employees, but also subordinate leaders from vice-presidents, directors, and managers to supervisors and team leaders. If you fit this profile, you are, regardless of your level or position, a leader of leaders. As such, you must expand the focus of your reflective attention to include the actions and behaviors of the leaders that report to you. Leaders of leaders bear special obligations and challenges, often without ever understanding it.

A quick story makes this clear. We once worked with a cheese manufacturing company that was trying to move from an authoritarian, top-down leadership style to one using much more employee participation. Brian, a manager of one of the larger plants, readily accepted the challenge of reframing his concept of leadership and was doing an extraordinary job of making new and unfamiliar choices. He was making remarkable strides in involving the people reporting directly to him, but one day we asked him how his subordinate supervisors were coming in their efforts to increasingly involve *their* people. Brian blanched and, after a moment's hesitation, said faintly, "That's part of my job, too?" Until that moment he had assumed that having his subordinate leaders attend the training he had was sufficient. He had not considered it to be part of his job to ensure that those supervisors took on the same challenges he did.

What Brian had failed to understand was that his role as a leader obliged him to expand the circle of his reflection. Leaders must establish clear leadership standards for subordinate managers and reinforce those expectations through training, coaching, and mentoring, as well as regular systems of feedback, encouragement, and recognition. They must pay attention not only to their own effectiveness as a leader, but also to the effectiveness of each leader within their scope of authority.

Put another way, leaders of leaders must manage leadership itself. This is a concept that is foreign to a surprising number of leaders. That blind spot contributes to many problematic organizational dynamics. To illustrate, as part of our formal organizational assessments we routinely ask employees to tell us what management is

> *Leaders of leaders must manage leadership itself. They must pay attention not only to their own effectiveness, but also to the effectiveness of each leader within their scope of authority.*

like in their organization. By far the most common response, regardless of organization size, industry, or the person's position or title, is, "It depends. It depends on who you work for. Some are great, and some are terrible."

The implication embedded in this response is that leadership goes unmanaged in those organizations. Leadership is allowed to be personality-based, with no overarching standards of organizational leadership and no clear systemic values or principles. In such organizations the quality of leadership that employees experience depends entirely on the supervisor to whom they report. Those lucky enough to work for top-notch leaders may enjoy fantastic working experiences. Those who have the misfortune to work for less effective leaders have experiences that range from disheartening to debilitating.

This range in the quality of leadership is so common and widespread that it is often assumed to be an inescapable fact of organizational life. Senior leadership seems willing to allow poor, counterproductive, and sometimes destructive leadership to continue for years and sometimes decades.

We still remember the time we sat in a CEO's office poring over survey data that indicated a huge variation in how supervisors and managers were perceived throughout the company. The CEO appreciated the usefulness of the survey process not only in identifying company-wide issues, but in pinpointing problem supervisors as well. We agreed but suggested that the situation was more complex than that. We brought his attention to data showing that three supervisors were doing a great job and three others were struggling or failing. All six of those supervisors reported to the same manager, who in turn reported to a plant manager, who reported to a vice president, who reported to the CEO himself. We pointed out that for this disparity of frontline leadership to exist, the overseeing manager had been asleep at the switch, as had the plant manager, and the vice president, and, ultimately, the president himself. He laughed and said, "I followed you right until that last point." Although he made a joke, we gave him credit for realizing that this inconsistency was due to his own lack of attention to leadership excellence throughout his organization. In short, he had allowed poor leadership to persist as long as reasonable production numbers were met.

All leaders must understand that a clear chain of impact, and therefore responsibility, stretches from themselves to the people at the front lines of their organizations. We once worked with the city manager of a mid-sized metropolitan area. To impress on him the systemic implications his choices had in building culture among his subordinate managers, we challenged him with the notion that if any night maintenance worker in the courthouse or city hall, any garbage collector or records clerk went home at the end of his or her shift feeling unvalued, unrecognized, unencouraged, or uninvolved, he, the city manager, was not doing his job effectively. He was not ensuring that the leadership system he headed was uniformly suffused with the elements needed for superior performance. He had not sufficiently driven the values of the targeted culture throughout the ranks of leadership and effectively engaged them to a point where they, along with himself, hung their respective mirrors and sincerely reflected on their leadership choices.

Edgar Schein, the expert on organizational culture quoted in chapter one, indicated that, based on his research and experience, the *primary* creator of an organization's culture is the behavior and choices of leaders. Recognizing this, leaders of leaders must understand that no targeted, systemic culture can be built without the unified commitment, full cooperation, and complete engagement of all the system's leaders. This is unquestionably challenging, but it is also an unparalleled opportunity. It allows the multiplication of constructive practices, thereby increasing the quality of functioning throughout an organization.

Expanding Your Focus – Engaging the Whole System

For many leaders, expanding their reflection to include other leaders requires a degree of reorientation about their responsibility. The next expansion of focus requires even more. It requires that leaders understand the responsibility they bear for the views, values, and choices of everyone who works within their span of authority, leaders and non-leaders alike. This does not imply that leaders must therefore become the behavior police. Far from it. Effective fulfillment of this responsibility cannot rely on the constant application of externally applied controls. Rather it requires the development and internalization by everyone of those values and attitudes that characterize the culture being targeted.

Leaders cannot create positive attitudes simply by ordering employees to adopt them. However, they can and must create a culture that engages people's participation and influences their thinking and behavior. This process begins by raising to a point of principle the way people value and treat each other. To expand on this, let us share the development of our own thinking in this regard.

For years we noticed that when people are asked about their job, they speak easily and at length about their job description and the technical tasks they perform. It is as if a job could be defined solely as *work done to achieve organizational objectives.* During the course of our twenty five years of organizational development work, however, it has become increasingly clear to us that this definition is not sufficient.

> *People in organizations don't work in isolation. They work in relationship with other human beings to achieve organizational objectives. The quality of those relationships, therefore, is part of a person's job, and one that leadership needs to elevate and highlight.*

People working toward organizational objectives don't work in isolation. They work *in relationship* with other human beings to achieve these objectives. This is what helped us realize that the quality of relationships is a significant part of a person's job, and one that leadership needs to elevate and highlight.

The importance of this human aspect of work, this "in-relationship," is almost universally overlooked. No one has ever, in all the years we have talked to people about their work, said that part of their job is to work effectively in relationship with other people. That we miss this crucial facet of our jobs, despite the fact that effective human relationships are a prerequisite of all successful human systems, goes a long way to explaining the root of many persistent organizational problems. Correcting this blind spot is where leadership becomes indispensable.

Leaders must ensure that the effectiveness of the interpersonal relationships in the system they lead becomes a collective priority, one that is vigorously pursued and reflected upon by all within the system. They must pay attention to the attitudes and choices made by everyone within their overall authority, resulting in each person reflecting on his or her own attitudes and choices. The goal is that all people will consider how they interact with others and whether those interactions further or hinder their organization.

Forging a Reflective Organization

Engaging everyone in this collective reflection is clearly a multifaceted process. Truly reflective organizations require the above forms of personal reflections to be accompanied by equally important mechanisms of collective reflection, whereby the system as a whole can be evaluated and the functioning of its constituent elements assessed and refined. Such reflection might consider the relationships between particular departments, the efficacy of systemic policies and procedures, the distribution of tasks and responsibility, or the flow of information from one organizational level to another.

To establish robust patterns of collective reflection, leaders must first ensure that data related to culture is collected. Such data allows the organization to put measures to the human aspect of organizational life and spot upward and downward trends, leading to corresponding celebration or focused attention and corrective action. Systemwide conversation about the results of the data ensures that reflection incorporates the insights and observations of all organizational levels, not just leadership. Leaders must then engage in and encourage widespread dialogue to assess collective efforts. This can take place informally and within regular, structured opportunities for analysis. Leaders must not only talk about the importance of collective reflection but also devote organizational time and resources to it.

And, just as an individual leader is wise to solicit the perceptions of other people, organizations may, periodically, also wish to seek assistance from an external resource to provide an objective assessment of its existing culture that can be combined with its own internal findings.

Strategies such as these establish reliable feedback loops that code purposeful and unified reflection into the DNA of an organization. Such habits of reflection ensure that whatever external challenges an organization might face, its internal functioning will enable it to continue to grow and develop. In a very real way the combined power of personal and collective reflection is the bedrock of continuous organizational im-

> *The combined power of personal and collective reflection is the bedrock of continuous organizational improvement.*

provement, and only through its agency can organizations hope to ensure the consistency of self-analysis and correction needed to maintain ever-improving systems.

Putting it All Together: Reflective Leadership, Reflective System

Every organization, no matter what its industry or constituency, exists to make some contribution to society, to meet some demand. It must, or it would have already given way to something that does, disappearing into the past like buggy whip manufacturers. Every organization has a purpose, and leaders are leaders only to the degree that they advance that purpose.

The challenge, then, is how do leaders – more specifically, how do *you*, as a leader – do this? Throughout this book we have considered elements that must inform any successful leadership approach. Among these were: recognizing the responsibility that comes with your organizational authority, consciously determining the direction of your organization's culture, respecting the human knowledge base, choosing positive and productive behaviors, evaluating your efforts through the perceptions of others, recognizing employees, involving employees in the decision-making process, creating a communication-rich culture, acknowledging the dignity and human worth of those around you, and listening with the intent to understand perspectives different than your own – all with an awareness of the below-the-line roots of your actions accompanied by honest reflection on the mindsets and values that shape everything you do as a leader.

This chapter and the previous one specifically asked you to focus your attention beyond yourself. Reflection cannot stop at your own personal level but must become an attribute of the entire human system you lead. This requires articulating a clear and emotionally resonant vision of the future, intentionally defining specific cultural values for your organization's internal functioning, and involving everyone within the organization in pursuing those vision and values. The extent to which your organization, then, collectively holds a mirror, assessing its alignment

> *Reflection cannot stop at your own personal level but must become an attribute of the entire human system you lead.*

with its own values in terms of both personal choices and organizational processes, will make all the difference in its long term capacity to achieve its potential.

The culmination of these diverse elements is a fully optimized system whose distinguishing feature is unity – a vibrant and conscious cohesion of aims, plans, and values. Unity is what will enable your organization to reflect productively on its performance and functioning, rather than splintering along lines of personal or organizational interests. Unity is crucial to collective excellence, and if you as a leader target it, plan for it, and practice it, you will put your organization on a path of continuous improvement.

Questions to Ponder – Whole System Reflection

- Is the leadership within my organization determined by personality or by knowledge and cultural values?

- Do I see it as an aspect of my leadership responsibility to create a system in which every leader reporting to me is hanging a mirror and practicing the discipline of reflective leadership? Do I manage leadership itself within my organization?

- Have I raised the way people treat one another to a point of principle in my organization? In what ways is attention paid to it? In what ways is it discussed?

- Do my employees see it as part of their job to engage with others effectively, in alignment with our stated cultural values?

- Do we have active, regular methods of gauging how well the operation of the organization truly reflects its values? Do we have methods of discovering contradictions between our stated organizational values and how the organization actually operates? Do we have regular methods of engaging all levels of the organization in conversation about how the culture can be improved?

Living the Reflective Life

The targets of reflection for effective leaders are numerous. The culture they are building, the vision they are crafting and communicating, the way they use authority, the way they communicate with employees, the extent to which they are respecting human dignity and worth, the efforts they are making to involve others, as well as the many attitudes and mental models that drive these actions – all of these require sustained thought and consideration. Clearly, reflection must be more than a sometimes-on, sometimes-off proposition.

Mindfulness and Meditation

How many times have you been in the car when, wrapped in thoughts of the day, you found yourself driving somewhere other than your destination? Such "autopilot" tendencies of defaulting to familiar routines in the absence of conscious thought have their use in life, not the least of which is enabling us to function in a highly multitasking world. But while auto piloting is obvious on the road, it is much harder to spot in daily interactions with others – and potentially much more detrimental.

Unless we are consciously and regularly reflecting on our beliefs, behaviors, and choices, we are almost assuredly following the well-worn paths of ingrained habit. This is not necessarily bad, for these routines might well yield generally acceptable results. Yet they will also ensure that our interactions with coworkers and employees end in the same places over and over again. If we wish to improve these interactions, if we wish to find new and more productive end points for our relationships, we must abandon the autopilot and make more intentional choices about what we are doing and where we are going.

Reflection is a condition that, at its heart, requires mindfulness. Mindfulness of this sort is an awareness of ourselves as we go about our day, an awareness not only of what we are doing, but why and how we are doing it. It requires us to be in the moment and to give attention to what is going on around and inside us *now*.

Achieving this kind of mindfulness requires detachment from one's self and a certain degree of distance from our personal thoughts, feelings, and desires. In a mindful and reflective attitude, we are not only taking part in the interaction of the moment – strategizing with a partner, clashing with a coworker – but we are also standing apart and at a distance. We are monitoring our proceedings with the eyes of a neutral observer rather than those of an invested participant.

If this sounds like a form of meditation, it is. Mindfulness and reflection are both expressions of a fundamentally meditative process, and both center on the removal of personal attachment to ideas, outcomes, and views as a means to achieve specific goals. In traditional forms of meditation that goal is enlightenment or connection with a higher being. In a framework of leadership the goal is connection with the human realities of a people-based organization (as all organizations ultimately are). Reflective leaders are, moment by moment, appraising their below-the-line values and beliefs and considering the way those mindsets affect the thinking, attitudes, morale, commitment, and vision of employees. They are working to understanding how the human spirit operates in their organization, how that spirit translates into concrete performance, and how they are furthering or hindering that spirit.

Many practitioners of traditional meditation would suggest that the practice's primary orientation is actually outwards, not inwards. The practitioner benefits, but the ultimate goal is developing the capacity to advance the well-being and prosperity of the world and its peoples. Reflective leadership is much the same. The leader reaps benefits, but the discipline is no mere self-help tool or strategy for personal improvement. Rather it is a practical means of optimizing the functioning of human systems. Leaders who understand their effect on the systems and interactions around them can best identify and achieve the changes needed to advance those systems. Ultimately, then, reflective leadership is a path to continuous organizational improvement.

The Roots of Reflection

By now it should be clear that reflection is, first and foremost, a below-the-line state of mind. Given that reflective leadership depends primarily on the interior landscape of the leader, having a firm grasp of the values that underlie a reflective life is imperative. The following characteristics, while by no means exhaustive, are among the more noteworthy.

Detachment

All of us are attached to particular views of the world and ways of approaching it. We know that a project is pointless, and we have no time for those who think otherwise. We know that a favored employee is a gem, regardless of performance reviews that suggest otherwise. We have our positions, and regardless of circumstances, we are committed to them. We are convinced. We are *sure*.

Attachment is a dangerous characteristic, especially for leaders. When we become attached to a certain idea, situation, or action, we care less about what is true, right, and useful than what will vindicate our position. Having invested ourselves in a particular point of view, we defend it not because of its merits but simply because it has become an extension of ourselves. We place ourselves in a position where our personal stature will be diminished if our chosen view is discarded or discredited, and we are therefore inclined to defend that view to the bitter end – a situation that becomes a recipe for disaster when parties become attached to opposing sides of the same issue.

Detachment is what allows leaders to escape from this counter-productive and ultimately artificial win/lose construct. When we are detached from an issue, we have a stake not in any particular side or philosophy, but rather in finding the best possible outcome. We are left free to explore facts and evaluate options with an unbiased mind, free to adjust our thinking as circumstances change and new facts come to light. We are free to objectively consider our positions and thinking, rather than being locked into positions rendered inflexible by personal attachments. Detachment, for leaders, is freedom.

Humility

Humility is one of the more nuanced characteristics of outstanding leaders. By definition, leaders have been placed above their employees in terms of organizational authority and responsibility. What, then, does humility look like in someone who necessarily oversees others?

Humility concerns the manner in which leaders approach their employees – the tone they take, the interaction they foster – but it also concerns the way leaders approach themselves. In this respect humility implies an unreserved acknowledgement of one's own limitations, shortcomings, and weaknesses. This acknowledgement includes both the challenges that are known to us (our "pet" vices) as well as those that exist in our blind spot. Humility is important because only by acknowledging areas in which we need improvement can that improvement actually be made. If we are convinced the problem lies elsewhere – the staff, the union, the marketplace – we will never become anything more than what we are right now.

In terms of the discipline of reflection, humility implies an acceptance that problems often emanate as much from us as they do from others. Our views, choices, or actions may be the root problem. Even when they are not, humility keeps us open to finding approaches that would be more constructive. Humility, at its highest, involves not just correcting deficiencies we may have, but actively searching for ways to improve our interactions. Eliminating negatives builds good organizations; cultivating positives – realizing there is always room for our own growth – builds outstanding ones.

Determination

Building reliable habits of reflection is not easy. Like mastering any new skill, learning to hang the mirror involves no small amount of setback and failure. We maintain a sense of objectivity and then lose it at a bad turn of events or a sharp verbal jab. We restrain emotional responses when the going is easy but lose our composure in the situations we most need it. We try, but we fall short, and we must either give up or keep pushing forward.

Training oneself to regularly and reliably hang the mirror is a process that tests a leader's resolve and resolution. Generating the determination needed to build productive patterns of behavior depends in large part on shifting from a focus on "getting it" to a focus on "getting closer to it." If we have never taken time to assess our interior landscape, taking a first look is a step in the right direction. A daily reflective practice that is fragile and easily interrupted is nevertheless a daily practice and a foundation from which to build. Slowly, with determination, our capacity for reflection can be strengthened and improved until we become able to reflect on our choices in real time, as we are making them. This condition – adopting more productive behavior on the spot, rather than after the fact – is, in a way, the final goal of a reflective discipline. But we can only achieve it through the fits and starts of determined effort.

Patience and Perseverance

Living in a culture of easy solutions and quick fixes, we all expect some degree of immediacy in our endeavors. We want the computers fixed now, not tomorrow, the paperwork completed yesterday, not today. Deep down, though, most of us know that very few things worth our time will happen overnight and without effort. Sudden transformation is possible, but real and sustainable development is reached only on a path built over months and years, one brick at a time.

If determination is critical to a reflective discipline, patience and perseverance are its twin sisters. Reflective leadership – indeed a reflective practice of any kind – is less about growing by leaps and bounds than pursuing a steady process of little-by-little, day-by-day. Leaders who are looking for the one-and-done answer will never find satisfaction in such a regimen – nor will they find success with it. But even leaders who knowingly commit to the rigors of a reflective path should not underestimate the patience they will need to have with themselves and others, nor the perseverance they will need to develop and exercise. Short-term success can be quickly won, but sustainable improvement is built only through patience and perseverance born of conviction.

Discipline and the Reflective Life

Throughout this book we have referred to the "discipline" of reflective leadership. Discipline is an interesting word. In one sense it refers to a particular subject or course of study, a branch of learning to be mastered. In the case of the discipline of reflective leadership, it refers to educating ourselves about the principles of the human knowledge base and reflecting on how our choices and behaviors, as perceived by those with whom we interact, conform to or violate those principles. Reflective leadership, in this sense, is a field that we both study and work to employ.

In another sense, though, discipline implies self-control and restraint. It suggests a standard we must strive to achieve, a path we must exert effort to follow. In this light, discipline becomes the final and preeminent characteristic of the reflective leader.

What does it mean to be disciplined in the pursuit of reflective leadership? It means we take reflection seriously. We strive to practice it in all cases, regardless of the external circumstances we face. We refuse our own exceptions and excuses, and reject our own justifications and explanations. We don't allow the situations we face – that we're sick and grouchy, that the pressure of a deadline is immense, that the predicament we're facing is unjust – to absolve us. We steadfastly keep our eyes fixed on ourselves and the choices we are making. We do this because these choices are where we have the greatest leverage and where the most improvement, both personal and organizational, will be achieved.

It is a basic human tendency to focus on the shortcomings and failures of others. Turning the weight of that critical gaze back on ourselves takes discipline and commitment. Keeping it there takes even more. But what is leadership if not the quest for continual improvement? Where will improvement come from, if not from leaders conscientiously hanging the mirror and giving honest consideration to what they see reflected back at them? Reflection is the surest means of development and growth, not only for leaders and managers but for human beings in any context. Only through reflection can we and those around us realize the potential that lies within. Only through reflection do we become everything we could be.

We wish you all the best.

Tools for Practicing the Discipline of Reflective Leadership

The questions to ponder at the end of each chapter are repeated here for ease of ongoing use. At the end, some further questions are included to stimulate your leadership reflection.

As we mentioned in the introduction, our intention in providing these questions is that they, and others like them, can be used again and again, until, hopefully, they become a natural part of hanging your leadership mirror.

Questions to ponder from the end of each chapter

Chapter 1 – Culture
- How would I describe the culture in which my employees work? How would my employees describe it? In what ways do our views differ?
- In what ways am I creating culture every day? What are my primary impacts on my organization's culture? What could I do or stop doing that would improve the culture?
- Is our culture distinguished by its excellence? Does it bring out the best in people? What conditions do I consciously create that cause employees to bring their best to the workplace?

- To what extent do I use my power and authority *for* my employees versus *on* them? How would my employees answer this question?

Chapter 2 – Below the Line

- What fundamental beliefs, attitudes, and assumptions shape my leadership philosophy and approach? How is my thinking reflected in my leadership actions?
- How open am I to the possibility that my attitudes and beliefs contribute to organizational difficulties?
- Which of my leadership actions and decisions might contradict the values and principles in which I say I believe? In what areas do the people around me, especially my employees, see contradictions between what I say and what I do?
- What could I do or stop doing to bring my actions more into conformity with my stated values? What below-the-line thinking would need to change in order for my actions to be more aligned with my stated values? How willing am I to take on those changes?

Chapter 3 – Knowledge, Choice, Perceptions

- How much of my leadership is supported by the knowledge base about how human beings act, react, and interact? How much is based on my personal preferences and reactions?
- How often are my leadership responses based on habit versus conscious, mindful choice?
- How would the people who observe me as a leader answer the above questions?

- Do I actively work to find out how employees perceive me as a leader? What methods do I use? How open am I to the feedback I receive? How effectively do I use it to grow as a leader?

Chapter 4 – Capturing the Human Spirit
- What do I believe causes employees to be motivated?
- What do I believe is my role in employee motivation? What leads me to believe this? Where do my beliefs come from, and upon what are they based?
- To what degree do I, as a leader, operate as if human beings are intrinsically self-motivated? To what degree do I operate as if people must be externally enticed or coerced into doing work?
- In what ways am I creating conditions that lead to employee motivation?
- What am I doing that might undermine employee motivation? What conditions have I created or allowed that may diminish employee motivation?
- How much do I rely on KITA-style management techniques to get people to work? How would my employees answer this question?

Chapter 5 – Vision
- What is my below-the-line thinking about the role of vision in organizational functioning? Do my leadership actions seem to indicate that I believe that employees can find opportunities for meaningful achievement without an understanding of the big picture surrounding their jobs?

- Do I have a compelling vision for the future of my organization? What is that vision?

- How consistently, and in what ways, does my vision impact my decisions, focus, actions, and use of time? How clearly do I think my employees see this vision reflected in my leadership choices and actions?

- How clearly would my employees be able to say what my vision is? To what degree do they understand it? To what degree do they have a collective sense of ownership of it?

- In what ways have I made vision a core element of my organization's culture? In what ways do we use the vision to determine actions, make decisions, formulate plans, and solve problems in our organization?

- To what degree does this vision create a context in which work is done and evaluated? In what ways do I explicitly connect employee's accomplishments with the achievement of the vision?

Chapter 6 – Recognition

- What do I believe are a leader's responsibilities in relation to appreciation and recognition? What do my actions in relation to recognition reveal about my thinking about the human beings I employ?

- To what degree do I truly appreciate the human beings working for me? In what ways do I express appreciation for the contribution of employees?

- How much do I rely on formal recognition programs, versus personal and/or informal expressions of recognition?

- What keeps me from expressing recognition and appreciation to employees more than I do? What elements of my below-the-line thinking in relation to recognition may need to change?

- Do my employees feel recognized and appreciated for their good work?

Chapter 7 – Involvement

- Do I believe that employee thinking is important to effectively solving organizational problems, making better decisions, and improving my own thinking? How clearly do I put that belief into practice on a daily basis?
- How much do employee opinions matter to me? Do I genuinely value the thinking of my employees to the point that I actively seek it out?
- Why don't I ask for employee input more than I do? How open am I to considering that my below-the-line thinking may need to change? In what ways may my thinking need to change?
- How much do I experience fears related to involvement such as surrendering authority and control, losing importance, being upstaged or outperformed by employees (and others listed on pp. 92 and 93)?
- In what ways am I creating conditions that lead to employees having a sense of ownership in their work? What am I doing that might undermine employee ownership?
- How would my employees answer the above questions?

Chapter 8 – Communication

- To what degree am I committed to building a communication-rich environment? What mechanisms and approaches do I use to create that environment? How successful are my efforts?

- Would my employees say they work within a communication-rich environment? Would they say they get all the information they need and would like? Do they feel they get the information in a timely and understandable way?

- How effectively do I communicate information related to specific content areas like vision, goals and objectives, feedback, job descriptions, policies and procedures, standards and expectations, organizational relationships and structures, and others (see p. 103)?

- How effectively do I communicate with my employees? Do I rely on one way communication? Do I engage employees in work-related dialogue and conversation?

- How would I honestly answer the questions (on pp. 115 and 116) inspired by the Hayakawa quote about listening?

- How important to me are protecting my employees' dignity and acknowledging their worth? How does this show in my daily behavior? Do my employees view me as a person committed to protecting their dignity and worth? Does my thinking need to change in relation to this topic?

- Do I listen to employees with a commitment to understanding frames of reference different than my own? Do my employees view me as an effective listener, committed to understanding what they are saying?

- How would I assessment myself in relation to the communication questions on pp. 119 and 120?

Chapter 9 – Personal Reflection

- How consciously do I take on the task of growth and self improvement as a leader?
- How does my commitment to leadership growth show itself?
- How often do I reflect on my leadership strengths and shortcomings?
- How do I go about seeking out external perceptions about how effective I am?

Chapter 10 – Unity and Cultural Values

- Do I believe that disunity is normal and inevitable in organizations, or that whole-system unity can be achieved if targeted?
- Do I believe that low-grade levels of disunity don't significantly inhibit system functioning or that high levels of unity are required for system optimization?
- Do I consistently work to reduce divisive aspects in our organization? How?
- Am I proactively working to build unity in our organization? How?
- What can I do to reduce competition and increase cooperation in our system?
- Does our organization have a clearly defined set of values? How much are they reflected in the way we operate? How effectively are they communicated and discussed?
- Do I engage in the hard work of incorporating these principles into my daily behaviors? Do I consistently exemplify the cultural values?
- How would my employees answer the above questions?

Chapter 11 – Whole System Reflection

- Is the leadership within my organization determined by personality or by knowledge and cultural values?

- Do I see it as an aspect of my leadership responsibility to create a system in which every leader reporting to me is hanging a mirror and practicing the discipline of reflective leadership? Do I manage leadership itself within my organization?

- Have I raised the way people treat one another to a point of principle in my organization? In what ways is attention paid to it? In what ways is it discussed?

- Do my employees see it as part of their job to engage with others effectively, in alignment with our stated cultural values?

- Do we have active, regular methods of gauging how well the operation of the organization truly reflects its values? Do we have methods of discovering contradictions between our stated organizational values and how the organization actually operates? Do we have regular methods of engaging all levels of the organization in conversation about how the culture can be improved?

More questions for exploring what you believe, below-the-line, about leadership:

- What do I believe is the purpose of leadership? Why? Where do those beliefs come from?

- How would I define "success" in leadership?

- On what beliefs do I base my leadership actions?

- What do I think are my top three challenges in becoming a better leader?
- What do I believe are the most important tasks of a leader?
- "Integrity" has been defined as having a highly refined sense of obligation. As a leader, what are my obligations to my employees? What do I believe a good leader is obligated to do, provide, communicate, create, establish, etc.?

Considering everything I have read in this book:

- What are the most important insights I have gained?
- What will be most challenging to me personally?
- In what ways might my leadership thinking, beliefs, or values need to change?
- In what ways might my leadership actions and behaviors need to change?
- What would I like my leadership legacy to be?

Attributions

Chapter 1

1. James L. Heskett, Thomas O. Jones, Gary W. Loveman, W. Earl Sasser, Jr., and Leonard A. Schlesinger, "Putting the Service-Profit Chain to Work," *Harvard Business Review*, (original March April 1994, HBR Classic 2008), pp. 164-174.

Chapter 2

2. Douglas McGregor, *The Human Side of Enterprise*, New York: McGraw Hill, 1960; see also John Schtogren, *Models for Management*, The Woodlands, TX: Woodstead Press, 1981, pp. 11, 19.

3. Chris Argris, *Reasoning, Learning, and Action: Individual and Organizational*, San Francisco: Jossey-Bass, 1982, p. 85; see also Chris Argris and Donald Schön, *Theory in Practice: Increasing Professional Effectiveness*, San Francisco: Jossey-Bass, 1974.

4. Warren Bennis, "A Conversation with Warren Bennis," *Behavior OnLine*, see also Warren Bennis, *On Becoming a Leader*, New York: Perseus Book Group, Basic Books, 2009.

Chapter 3

5. Viktor Frankl, *Man's Search for Meaning*, Boston: Beacon Press, 2006

Chapter 4

6. Frederick Herzberg, "One More Time: How Do You Motivate Employees?" *Harvard Business Review*, (original January February 1968, HBR Classic 2003).

Chapter 5

7. Warren Bennis and Patricia Ward Biederman, *Organizing Genius: The Secrets of Creative Collaboration*, Boston: Addison Wesley, 1997, p. 23.
8. Peter Senge, *The Fifth Discipline*, New York: Doubleday, 1990, p. 206.
9. John Kotter, "Leading Change: Why Transformation Efforts Fail," *Harvard Business Review*, (original March April 1995, HBR Classic 2007).

Chapter 6

10. Marcus Buckingham and Curt Coffman, *First Break All the Rules*, New York: Simon and Schuster, 1999, p. 28.
11. Frederick Herzberg, "One More Time: How Do You Motivate Employees?" *Harvard Business Review*, (original January February 1968, HBR Classic 2003).
12. Scott Adams, *The Dilbert Principle: A Cubicle's-Eye View of Bosses, Meetings, Management Fads & Other Workplace Afflictions*, New York: HarperCollins, 1996, p. 33.

Chapter 7

13. Jay Hall and Martha S. Williams, "Group Dynamics Training and Improved Decision Making," *Journal of Applied Behavioral Science*, (March 1970, vol. 6).

Chapter 8

14. Victor H. Vroom and John G. Searle, "Educating Managers for Decision Making and Leadership," *Management Decision*, (2003).
15. S. I. Hayakawa, "How to Attend a Conference," *The Use and Misuse of Language*, Fawcett Premier, 1962, p. 70.
16. Peter F. Drucker, *Management: Tasks, Responsibilities, Practices*, New York: HarperCollins, 1974.

Chapter 10

17. Alfie Kohn, *No Contest: The Case Against Competition*, New York: Houghton Mifflin, 1986.

CPSIA information can be obtained at www.ICGtesting.com
Printed in the USA
LVOW061414171012

303215LV00002B/67/P

9 781600 477584